# HIGH-RISK TRAINING

Managing Training Programs for High-Risk Occupations

# GARY WARD

# HIGH-RISK TRAINING

## Managing Training Programs for High-Risk Occupations

**NP**

Nichols Publishing/New York
Kogan Page/London

First published in 1988 by Nichols Publishing,
P.O. Box 96, New York, NY 10024

Books bearing the Nichols Publishing imprint are published by GP Publishing, Inc.

**Library of Congress Cataloging-in-Publication Data**
Ward, Gary, 1942-
   High-risk training : managing training programs for high-risk occupations /
Gary Ward.
        p.       cm.
   Includes index.
   ISBN 0-89397-298-3
   1. Employees, Training of—Management.    I. Title.
HF5549.5.T7W36  1988
658.3′12404—dc19                                                                87-31332
                                                                                                CIP

Published in the United Kingdom by Kogan Page, Ltd, 120 Pentonville Road, London
N1 9JN

**British Library Cataloguing in Publication Data**
Ward, Gary
   High-risk training: managing training programs for high-risk occupations.
   1. Personnel. Training. Management aspects
   I. Title.
   658.3′ 124

   ISBN 1-85091-670-5

Printed and bound in the United States of America
94 93 92 91 90 89 88                    5 4 3 2 1

# Contents

# Figures

# Preface

During a quarter century of work in technical training, I read every book I could find on the subject. The books seemed to fall into two categories. One type was written by retired training managers who described how to do what they had been doing. Although there were always useful tips in each book, their recommended practices never seemed to travel well into the organizations where I worked. The narrow programs they described would not mesh with the parts I already had in place.

I had a similar experience with the other category of books on training, the research-based, university-originated books. Somewhere inside the inevitable seven models in each book, there were a few useful bits of information. Again, the many untried processes they recommended were narrow in scope and would not fit. I am a trainer, not a researcher. I had neither the time nor the resources to field test their ideas.

I finally decided both categories of books had two things in common. One was their view of training. It was as if they were watching the Rose Bowl game from the Goodyear blimp without electronic aids. Each expert concentrated on how to best play one position on the team. Furthermore, and this is the second thing they had in common, their recommendations were to rebuild the entire program around their one favorite position.

The situation is different now. We trainers are in the stands and can see all the pieces go together. We are in the stands because we have a field-proven technology of training. This science of training allows training managers, supervisors, and senior decision makers to make sense out of the movements on the field. The technology of training shows how to identify strengths and weaknesses and manage people, processes, and things toward success. Each unique training environment dictates the pace. Success occurs because of the scientific base—a base that has the beauty and wonder of working in most situations.

My main purpose in writing this book has been to share the technology, the science, that causes people to learn the right things and apply what they learn on the job. Moreover, I hope this book will make a major contribution to the recognition of trainers as professionals. The book pulls everything together into formal management systems that require skill and thoughtful handling by professionals. Everything is here; the book presents a full-scope approach that can be learned. There are no formal licenses, certificates, or degrees in training, but there are results. And results can be achieved by training professionals who master the principles in this book.

There is one more reason I wrote this book. In my twenty-five years in the business, I excelled for only the last six years. As the manager of nuclear training at one of the world's largest nuclear reactors, I finally achieved success. Success that brought compliments, accolades, and awards from regulatory agencies, industry groups, and professional organizations. In many ways, I owe this book to those who suffered with me during the preceding nineteen years. Accordingly, this book is dedicated to the late Pete Chapman, who saw promise in my early years; the memory of Sergeant Terry R. Corsen, USMC, who paid the price of my middle years; and Jack Calhoun, who trusted me in my later years.

To the following individuals, I offer my warm appreciation for their assistance: Helenanne Bendik, Len Boswell, Ellen Bowers, Ruth Cargo, Bob Healy, Tony Henson, Marilyn Lynch, Dan Poling, Bill Spence, Bill Stevenson, Cade Ward, Justin Ward, and Sharon Ward. I must also express my appreciation to the following organizations: NASA Flight Training Division, Johnson Space Center, Houston, Texas; First Strategic Aerospace Division (SAC), Vandenberg Air Force Base, Lompoc, California; Naval Training Center, Orlando, Florida; United Airlines, Cockpit Resource Management, Littleton, Colorado; Pennsylvania State University, State College, Pennsylvania; and Oklahoma State University, School of Occupational and Adult Education, Stillwater, Oklahoma.

Mountaintop, PA
October 1987

# Introduction

In our race to proudly enter the twenty-first century, we are daily faced with challenges—challenges that are old and new, challenges that excite us. We are a culture oriented to problem solving. We deserve the title of problem seekers. Our heritage is to find a problem, solve the problem, and move on to the next problem. The problem is, we have not been doing too well.

Our failures are broadcast around the world. We really do not mind some of our failures. When a piece of hardware fails in a new technology, we recover from our losses and set out to make the technology work. It is a great challenge, the type we seek. However, when failure is caused by human error, we are stunned. We should not be. As problem seekers, we sometimes have more confidence than common sense.

High-risk endeavors, whether old (a police officer on a beat) or new (gene splicing in a sterile laboratory), are still people based. People make technology work—people in the control rooms of nuclear power plants, people in the cockpits of commercial airlines, people behind the controls of a missile, people programming a supercomputer for a worldwide business venture, people operating a chemical processing plant, people making triage decisions in a hospital emergency ward, people operating rapid-transit systems. People make high-risk endeavors work or fail.

We have learned some hard lessons in the last two decades about human errors—from Three Mile Island to Chernobyl, from the Challenger explosion to one commercial air disaster after another, from the chemical leaks in Bhopal to chemical leaks in West Virginia, from Marines in Beirut to sailors in the Persian Gulf. Yet, we do not have to live and die that way. People do not want to make an error that could cost their lives, or the lives of others, or result in catastrophic loss of data and resources.

We must face the reality of the failures of our traditional training and education programs, and we must recognize that there is a better way. The better way is the scientific training of people to apply correct knowledge and skills in their work. We do not need to throw out everything that we have in place. But we do need to develop and implement training programs that *cause* the proper knowledge and skills to be both taught and applied on the job. We must put in place a technology of training that makes training fulfill its mission.

The purpose of this book is to illustrate how to develop, implement, and control a no-nonsense, get-it-done system of training that causes—yes, *causes*—effective on-the-job work. This book presents a full-scope demonstration of how to build or retrofit an existing training program without tearing the guts out of the good parts. It is specifically targeted at training managers and the supervisors and senior decision makers who are responsible for training. As a true science, the technology of training can be used in almost any environment. You only need to judge how much management control over training is needed, and then you can modify the management systems in this book to fit the local environment. But do not back the systems down too far. Everyone needs to reduce human error, and the rate of human error is inversely proportional to the degree of management control over training.

This book is divided into three major parts to correspond to the three spheres of management expertise that training leaders need: developing, implementing, and evaluating. They need to apply these managerial skills in the four areas of curriculum, staff, procedures, and records. Part 1, Developing, demonstrates how to develop curriculum, staff, procedures, and records. Part 2, Utilizing, shows how to implement and utilize curriculum, staff, procedures, and records. Part 3, Evaluating, directs how to evaluate curriculum, staff, procedures, and records. In addition, Part 4, Training through Simulation, presents a specialized approach to simulation learning. Simulation is the new wave in training and has impressive learning results.

Much of this book is based on concepts that have withstood the test of time. The problem is that we have made many of our concepts too complicated. Throughout the book, diagrams of the root meaning of key terms are presented to direct our thinking back to some central truths that we have overdefined, overworked, and thus undercommunicated. For example, how many definitions have you learned for the concept of management? Originally, the term was simple, easy to understand, and easy to communicate—

| MAN | AGE | MENT |
|:---:|:---:|:---:|
| ↓ | ↓ | ↓ |
| PEOPLE | + TIME → | CONCRETE RESULTS |

The original meaning of the concept wasn't bad. Neither is its application to high-risk training (HRT).

Everything you need is here in this book, from A to Z. So, let's get it done. Let's apply man-age-ment to HRT.

# Part 1: Developing

What is the foundation of the technology of training? The management processes used to *develop* curriculum, staff, procedures, and records. Decisions made about development set the course for success by dictating how you are going to do the business of training. How do you decide what content is most worth including in a training curriculum? What is most worth learning? How do you develop job experts into skilled trainers who cause learning to occur and are able to create quality training materials and scenarios? How do you manage their activities (and everything else)? What kinds and how many written controlling procedures do you need? How are procedures developed, approved, and revised? Once the procedures are in place, how do you know the procedures are followed? What needs to be tracked and recorded? How do you set up and operate a valid and reliable records system that will perform these tasks?

Part 1 answers these questions and many more by taking each of four areas and demonstrating how to accomplish development. Chapter 1, What You Need to Know, sets the stage for the book and shows the need for HRT methods by going through eight common pitfalls that face training professionals. Chapter 2, Developing Curriculum, is the *must-know* chapter of this book. Once you understand the scientific approach to developing training curriculums, the remainder of the book folds into place, chapter after chapter, building toward efficiency, effectiveness, and success. Chapter 3, Developing Staff, covers staff development and challenges you to enhance your own leadership skills. Chapter 4, Developing Procedures, is a nuts-and-bolts approach to developing, approving, updating, and controlling written procedures for the training function. Chapter 5, Developing Records, rounds out the development portion of the book by showing how to decide which data require documentation and how to establish a records management system.

Chapters 2 through 5 abound with easy-to-follow tables, graphs, matrices, and procedures. Study them carefully. Each carries a message on management, presents key training concepts, and provides a model that can be modified to fit your organization's needs.

# 1
# What You Need to Know

You need to know only three things to develop and manage training programs that prepare people for work that could cost their lives or the lives of others, or result in catastrophic losses of resources and data:

- how to *develop* curriculum, staff, procedures, and records;
- how to *utilize* curriculum, staff, procedures, and records;
- how to *evaluate* curriculum, staff, procedures, and records.

This book tells you how to do these things—these and many more—in detail, step by step. The processes are here: the tools, the techniques, the devices, the timing, the options. You'll find them in chapters 2 through 13. And you'll find more in chapters 14 through 16, on effective simulation training. Chapter 17 will help you put high-risk training (HRT) into action in your organization

Are these things hard to learn? Absolutely not. The one thing high-risk trainers have in common is that they didn't plan to be a trainer. Everyone has to learn on the job. There are no college degrees or continuing education programs in this field. If other trainers can do it, you can do it. That is, you can do it if you take the job one step at a time, monitor your results, and understand what works in your high-risk training program.

If high-risk training is so simple, why do the postmortems of disasters show that training was part or all of the problem? There are many examples of such disasters—Chernobyl, the Challenger, Bhopal, the Marines in Beirut, the Navy in the Persian Gulf, Three Mile Island—as well as the daily life-taking events in the transportation industry, emergency wards, and law enforcement.

High-risk training can fail when trainers fall into traps that disable the people trained. There are eight pitfalls in high-risk training:

1. Failing to take training seriously
2. Allowing senior decision makers to discount training
3. Deciding training starts and stops at the facility door
4. Electing to teach adults like children
5. Evaluating trainees too timidly
6. Ignoring the technology of training
7. Concentrating on things rather than people
8. Defending the perimeter

Every one of these traps can be a major hazard. Before we get down to specific training competencies, let's consider the effects of each pitfall in detail.

*Pitfall Number One: Failing to take training seriously.* You're reading this because you are a trainer or want to be a trainer or because you have made a leadership commitment to learn about training. Before you decided to become involved with training, who did you send to training when the quotas came out—your best, or the ones you could spare? Did you ever cancel or delay a program? What was your opinion of people who worked in training—did you see them as producers or as people who couldn't hold other jobs? How many programs did you attend that wasted your time, were out of date, or were run by people who couldn't teach? Can you take training seriously?

Poor training causes people to die, ruins careers, costs megabucks, and makes our society question our ability to manage and compete using new technologies (and some old ones). Scheduling people into a simulator to get their quarterly requirements out of the way is not good enough. Nor is training people to a level of blind confidence without ensuring competency. To be successful you must adopt a philosophy, belief, value, or attitude that says, "Training is serious business!"

New technology is the future. Competitiveness means more than a tough state of mind and physical strength on the playing field; it relates to how well we use technology. Technology— our machines and processes—is always changing to allow us to be more competitive. It doesn't matter whether we're training physicians to compete against death, soldiers to maintain the smart weapons, agents to battle organized crime, scientists to control the release of bioengineering products, truck drivers to haul hazardous waste, or computer experts to design programs for a global business venture. We're after the competitive edge that will allow us to move proudly into the twenty-first century with a high standard of living, with trust in technology, and with our freedoms intact.

Training is one way to gain trust in technology. We must gain the trust not only of the people who allocate dollars for new technology but also of the members of our society who protest new technology, for they can stop or retard technology.

And we must hold the trust of the people who work in new technology. If those who work with it don't trust new technology, then we will lose competitiveness.

Training is serious business for each individual, too. It's been a long time since a person could take one job and make it a career. Job change is a way of life, and training is the way to job change. According to the Carnegie Commission Report on Training in the United States, American businesses and industries spend more money each year on training than all the colleges and universities in the country. That amount doesn't include money invested by local, state, and federal agencies and the armed forces. Training is a big and growing business.

The futurist Alvin Toffler foresees that the workweek will soon be twenty-five hours, of which at least five hours will be spent in training. A twenty-five hour workweek—is that believable? Who would have believed a forty-hour workweek at the end of World War II? Toffler says:

> Workers are no longer interchangeable like so many parts on an assembly line. The challenge today is to train workers in new and continuously changing skills. Companies must adapt to greater competition in the world by cultivating innovation with training.

Failing to take training seriously is an easy trap; you've had some experiences that have left a bad taste. Try it, however— try taking training seriously. Remember one thing: no matter how bad or good things are at any given point, you can make things better.

You have to help others remember the importance of training. Sometimes they forget or deny its importance, too.

*Pitfall Number Two: Allowing senior decision makers to discount training.* Observe Fred X, formerly a six-year member of the "nuclear" navy, who at a young age worked his way up to the job of vice president of nuclear operations of one of the nation's largest nuclear power generating stations. He has a simple response when people ask him how he got so far so fast: "Hard work. Work as hard as I did, and you could be here."

Interesting. Fred X learned about his field through navy training. His transition to civilian nuclear power was aided and bolstered by training. His progress up the ladder was accompanied by training. Yet, to hear Fred X tell it, he was born with the knowledge: "Training? Oh yes, I had some; but hard work is the key."

Who among us would want to admit that we were not the main reason for our success? Maybe Fred X is the one who was born to success. Mostly though, Fred X is a problem because he denies the value of training, wants everyone else to do it the "hard way," and he approves the training budget. Fred X is not that different from many other senior decision makers, just a bit more outspoken and opinionated.

Here is a desperate pitfall for a training program. When training management allows senior management to forget the contribution training made to their career and to the successes of an ongoing business, the training budget will suffer, and the competency of the work force will decline. And—*never forget*—when an accident happens that was caused by human error, it will be the fault of training management.

Nice dilemma, isn't it? You can tell Fred X that he's an arrogant———. But if you do, you'll watch the training function deteriorate while waiting for the accident that will cost you your job and reputation, or even worse, kill somebody, force the company into hard economic times, scare the residents near the nuclear plant half to death, and bring out the protestors (who should rightfully be there in this case). Furthermore, media attention will not be favorable.

As a result, trust in technology is lost. If we can't manage a nuclear plant, space program, or chemical plant, how will we manage the technologies of the future, namely, biotechnology, nuclear medicine, and super-computer-controlled communications? What happens to our competitiveness, our standard of living, and our ability to protect ourselves?

All this because Fred X was arrogant? No. Training management fell into the trap—a trap that could have been avoided. The avenue is not to justify training the same way you would the costs and benefits of a new piece of hardware on a production line. Some of the outcomes of training are too nebulous to stand up in a cost-effectiveness budget battle against items that show an immediate return on dollars invested.

How can you make the case for training? In general, there are four ways to get people to do what you believe should be done in an organization:

- *Authority.* You give directions that are carried out.

- *Power.* You say, "Do it, or I will. . . ."

- *Persuasion.* You present logical arguments and gain a negotiated settlement.

- *Training.* You indoctrinate the person to believe and perform.

Let's look at each of these approaches.

Certainly you have no *authority* over senior management, unless you have a strong charter approved by the board of directors, training mandated by a law, or maybe the impetus of a committee in Congress. It could happen, but it's not likely. Authority is what you have over people who work for you (or perhaps what they give you).

*Power* falls into about the same category. Although you have power over someone who works for you who resists compliance, it's hard to fire your boss. You might threaten to go over the person's head, call the media, or put a letter in the files, but such power plays are not really recommended. A letter to the file and notes in the office calendar might, however, be helpful at some future time. But, overall, this strategy is not productive. It is just insurance.

*Persuasion* is the most common method of trying to get senior decision makers to come around. What type of logical argument would you present to them? How would you present your case to compete for funds? "Training is good. We need more training. New people aren't trained. We have a new piece of hardware and need training," and so forth. You can try simple persuasion, but don't count on a high success rate.

After reading this book, however, you will be able to develop a complete training program, demonstrate its contribution, and show how the trainees will be different after the training. There are no shortcuts; it takes work. For even though you may be a great speaker and negotiator and have other terrific qualities, if you haven't got the goods, you can't sell the program. You have to know the territory, the technology of training.

Then there is *training* as the fourth way. You must train (dare the word *educate* be used?) senior decision makers on the complexities, difficulties, costs, and contributions of training. You're a trainer. Do what you do best: train. Indoctrinate seniors with the values of training.

After reading this book, you will be competent to train senior decision makers about the contents, costs, and benefits of quality training. You will be able to back up your training requests by laying on the desk solid programs that prove the demand for training, specifically list the job tasks to be taught, associate a cost to each task, and document the benefits to the organization.

Keeping senior decision makers firmly behind training is a continuous job. And you can't do it from inside the training facility, which is the next pitfall to avoid.

*Pitfall Number Three: Deciding training starts and stops at the facility door.* Mary Y is a well-organized training director at a major hospital. She is responsible for the physicians, nurses, technicians, and the sanitation training for food service and maintenance personnel. She also provides orientation for the candy stripers.

Mary Y used to be a nurse, a career she decided to follow when she was eleven years old. She wanted to help people. The reality of nursing was different than she had imagined. Patient care was all right, but the physicians intimidated her. She was scared of them, and every time they would "sharpen their teeth" on her, she would go to pieces. She needed the job, so she stayed with it until a training slot opened.

Over time, she worked her way up to director. Mary Y took excellent care of the training rooms. She kept charts on each person and made certain their required training was up to date. No one had their license or certificate expire under Mary's directorship. Mary Y read all the right journals, kept the audiovisual materials current, and even attended a workshop on compact-disc, computer-based training.

Mary Y was still afraid of the physicians and head nurses. She would only walk the halls when she had to go to a meeting. In meetings, she would shake her head yes and agree to everything the physicians, head nurses, and administrator wanted, hoping they would forget or not follow up.

Yes, she probably knew that twenty-five thousand people die needlessly in emergency wards each year. Yes, she probably knew that health professionals have a rate of addiction to drugs and alcohol several times higher than the normal population.

Yes, she probably knew the handling of isotopes in nuclear medicine was not in accordance with the Nuclear Regulatory Commission's rule. Yes, she probably knew the hospital should have an emergency drill with the people at the new chemical plant south of town, but that was the administrator's problem.

Training stopped and started at the door to the training room where the schedule was always neatly posted. Even with the training Mary Y did coordinate, she never went onto the floors, into the operating rooms, down to the cafeteria, or to the emergency ramp to see if people were implementing the training. She never did a job analysis, a work practices observation, or a well-thought-out proposal on changing the state licensing rules to make training more meaningful. So, the hospital never bettered its triage ability in the emergency ward, never had a continuous behavioral observation program, never improved its isotope handling, and never did the emergency drill.

Mary Y got by with that—and management let her—until a lawsuit came from the emergency ward, with a patient dead and a physician's career over; until the anesthesiologist (hooked on fentanyl) overdosed a baby; until the NRC conducted an audit resulting in a shutdown penalty and fine; until there was a leak at the chemical plant. Mary Y let people with more status and rank intimidate her, and she and everyone else paid. It's a common occurrence. Our culture tends to allocate intelligence to senior decision makers and assume they know what we know.

Don't fall into the trap. Hospital administrators are hired to make sure that the physicians don't order another x-ray machine when there are two in the basement; senior military officers have been around longer; corporate executives have their own agendas filled with finance and policy; law enforcement leaders must live in the political world. Don't keep your training expertise hidden away from them. Senior decision makers want, need, and appreciate the input of HRT managers. This book gives you the strategies. You don't have to be Clint Eastwood to make your point with senior management. You do have to observe, think, and use the strategies in this book. Knowing how adults learn will help.

*Pitfall Number Four: Electing to teach adults like children.* The trainees in HRT do not come into the programs with blank spaces in their minds like grade school students. They have been through a screening and testing process, and most have previous experience, training, and education. They may have been in the business longer than you.

Adults don't learn. They relearn! They come to training with an idea already in place in their minds on what you are going to teach. And they believe in what they know; it's their reality. Ask any one hundred adults how good they are at their work, and ninety of them will put themselves in the upper quartile of competency.

Dr. Mac Z, a Ph.D. in physics, reluctantly resigned his position at the university to, as he explained to his colleagues, "help out the industrial world." Yes, they really needed him (besides, it doubled his salary). He came to the training center, and week after week lectured on basic physics to the engineers who passed through his class. When he saw a frown on a face in the neatly aligned classroom chairs, he would leave his podium, dash to the white board, and draw out an explanation. The whole experience was wonderful. He was saving the industry. Dr. Z was in rapture. All the engineers made good scores on his written test. By George, was he doing a good job!

Dr. Z had two problems. First, you don't teach experienced adults with a standard lecture. You first challenge their reality, what they think they know. Their idea of what you're going to teach is like a nice big round ball in their mind. You have to force them to recognize there are holes in it. If you can't—and they're right—you're teaching the wrong thing, something they already know. Second, assuming you are teaching them something they need to know, you don't treat experienced adults like kids in a classroom.

This book is filled with ways to challenge their realities. It can help you. It can help Dr. Z with his first problem, but not his second. You can teach something you don't know as well as you can come back from some place you've never been. Dr. Z is okay to teach beginners the parts of theory they need to know, but Dr. Z will never be satisfied until he has replicated Physics 101 in the training center, which would be a waste of money. So is the entire training program unless it properly evaluates the trainees.

*Pitfall Number Five: Evaluating trainees too timidly.* Taking something simple and making it hard doesn't make it good, nor does taking something hard and making it simple make it good. Both are a crime. Always have performance tests. Whenever possible, make the trainees show they can perform. Unless you see their performance, you don't know if they can do the work, if you've taught them something, changed them (which is the purpose of training). Take these examples.

As a Corporal, Gunnery Sergeant T, USMC, a combat engineer, disarmed more than fifty antipersonnel and antivehicular land mines in Vietnam. Assigned as lead instructor at the Combat Engineers School at Camp Lejeune, North Carolina, he was presented the challenge of cross-training eight infantry lieutenant colonels. He took them through everything except the simulated mine field where they would have to probe for and disarm mines. The mines would not blow up but would shoot a little dye on them if they failed. The gunnery sergeant could not bring himself to do that to colonels. His rationale was simple—"They'll never have to do it. Troops do that."

An Air Force general flew from Washington, DC, with his wife and a few officers for a civilian ceremony in Pennsylvania. He ran the plane off the end of the runway and killed everyone aboard. Pilot error. The last time he'd been in the flight simulator, his training had been supervised by a major. Around the world daily, senior flight officers are allowed to do less on simulators than people of the same or a lower rank than the instructors. In the military, on police forces, in nuclear power facilities, intimidation happens all the time.

Performance evaluations are insurance. If you can't do it for real, do it in simulation. This book tells you how. It encourages you to save lives by quality evaluation of performance. But, remember, performance evaluations are a part— but only a part—of the technology of training.

*Pitfall Number Six: Ignoring the technology of training.* Pity Bill Heavy. Bill is a new training manager who inherited the job. He's at the height of happiness because he goes to all the meetings with the big boys and can issue memos to his staff. Bill Heavy is perfectly content to hold the training manager's position until he retires in twenty-five years. Training is easy work, he thinks, a no-pressure job.

Yet he knows he has to do something new every once in a while to keep the job that long. He secretly ordered a twelve-dollar book from the *New York Times* classified section that would give him all the secrets. Little did he know that it was the one and only ad placed by a vanity press to satisfy an old college professor from the Midwest who'd paid to have his book published; the book was worth about twelve cents to Bill.

He continued his hunt for magic secrets while he attended meetings and wrote memos. He had a childlike faith in finding the hidden formula. He didn't want to be wrong, so he didn't do anything, while he insisted on trying to learn adult training the hard way. He decided to manage training by issuing rules on how instructors should behave in the classroom. He then audited the instructors against his rules and wrote more memos. Bill was happy, and management was happy because they received all the great audit discrepancy reports. Bill was sure working hard.

The only people who knew training wasn't going right were the trainees. No one ever asked them.

No such key to training exists. There aren't any formulas or secrets. At least no single secret. There is a technology, which this book presents. And although there may be something called a one-minute manager (doubtful), there can never be a one-minute trainer (guaranteed). Anyone who thinks there's a shortcut to high-risk training will be going to some funerals.

Yet some people like inanimate objects, and concentrate on things rather than on what makes technology work, people.

*Pitfall Number Seven: Concentrating on things rather than people.* M. Lite started out as a test engineer and ended up as a training manager with several simulators. He knew where his success lay, in making those simulators work. Instructors be damned; software engineers were what (who) was needed. Without field-experienced instructors, however, no one knew if the simulators worked or not. The software people said so. They should know, simulators are only computers anyway. "Touch, what does that mean? Feel? The gauges work. Sounds? We want it quiet for training; besides, the software people can't work with noise out here."

Technology consists of people, processes, and things. All are important. Concentrate only on things or processes, and failure occurs automatically. Concentrate on people, and there is a potential for success.

*Pitfall Number Eight: Defending the perimeter.* Enter Captain Strong, the second most-decorated highway patrolman on active duty, to take over the Academy. Captain Strong knows exactly what each graduate should know, be able to do, and look like. He rips apart the existing curriculum and bulldozes his curriculum into place. Whenever anyone inside the Academy questions the curriculum, he looks patiently at them, then explains in a fatherly fashion that he's been there and knows best. When officers outside the Academy make suggestions or complain about the quality of the graduates, he shouts about his prowess as a highway patrolman.

The Academy was no longer the highway patrol's, it was Captain Strong's. It didn't take long for each barrack in the state to establish its own bootlegged training program. Efficiency for the entire state went down because the operating units had to invest in initial training.

Captain Strong looked at himself as a highway patrolman, not a trainer. He didn't see the Academy as a service support unit for the operating force. He froze out those who could help, and everyone suffered. No one would want Captain Strong to forget he was an experienced law enforcement officer, but he needed to remember that he was a trainer.

This chapter was meant to challenge your reality. It was a purposeful act. Did you learn? Did you recognize the eight traps?

The price for not knowing how to develop and manage high-risk training programs is high. Stuff a Marine into a body bag sometime, and live with the knowledge that he didn't have to die. Go to the wake of your law enforcement neighbor. Lay on the table in an emergency ward and wonder.

You don't have to pay that price. You can do something about the waste. If there is a key to training, it's in chapter 2—deciding what's most worth knowing by the trainee. Chapter 2 is the core, the foundation of training. Work it through, and the remainder of the book will fold in, layer by layer, tier by tier.

# 2
# Developing Curriculum

Training programs are always limited by time, money, hardware, software, facilities, instructors, staff members, and the level of competencies of incoming trainees. Within these boundaries, training managers have the responsibility to concentrate training programs on the "things most worth knowing." Many times training management is a race.

This chapter presents ways to win the curriculum part of the race, through knowledge of the concept of curriculum, levels of curriculum, functions of two curriculum models, a curriculum data tracking system, and curriculum revision strategies. But, first, let's look at what we mean by *concept*.

A concept is an abstraction with a specific definition. Any recognizable order of symbols, letters, or numbers will bring a thought to mind. One example is money. The symbols that make up the word *sunrise* bring a visual concept to mind. $E = mc^2$ brings a different level of thought to mind. If the order of the symbols is unrecognizable ($\Sigma^p_{j=1} C_{ij} C_{kj}$) or brings multiple thoughts to mind (as in the concept of love), confusion results.

What does *curriculum* bring to mind? For success, you must have a clear concept and be able to teach others. If not, curriculum development will suffer from the classic lack of communication.

## Curriculum Concept

There are two problems with trainers and their concepts of curriculum. One group has more definitions of curriculum than Eskimos have for ice (Eskimos have dozens of words to describe different kinds of ice, which confuses outsiders). The other group of trainers doesn't have a concept of curriculum. Communicating the concept to them is like talking to tribesmen in the deep Sahara about ice.

Curriculum is a word borrowed from the ancient Romans. A *curricle* was a two-wheeled carriage drawn by two horses in side-by-side positions. This vehicle, obviously, led to chariot racing, running—a *currere*—of chariots over a track (a course). The second part of the word is even easier. *Clum* originally described the growing of a particular type of grass. It came to mean developing:

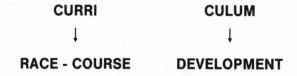

| **CURRI** | **CULUM** |
|:---:|:---:|
| ↓ | ↓ |
| **RACE - COURSE** | **DEVELOPMENT** |

Curriculum is the race (experiences) you put people through for their learning. Curriculum development is designing—siting if you will—where the racetrack shall go. Where shall it be wide, or narrow, or steep, or flat? Slow, fast, deep, or shallow? The track lays across the countryside. It uses the terrain, goes where the challenges of hills, swamps, valleys, and flatlands are needed to get the racers to the finish line. Some of the racers will probably fall out. If they can't take the track, they can't handle what lies beyond the finish line. Yet, we do not lay the track where it is all uphill. We lay it where it is needed to prepare the racers for the future beyond the finish line.

Each time the contour of the track changes significantly, we draw a line across the track and call it a course. The development of a course is the refining of the exact contours and boundaries of that section of the track. The track is continuous; the courses are well-articulated segments.

Laying out a racetrack cannot be done alone. Unless you explain the concept of track development (curriculum development) to the people who are working on the track, you will suffer, not benefit, from their expertise. You must help them understand the concept of curriculum, or you will end up with one of the following types of curriculum:

- *Traditional.* A horseracing track is usually circular and level and divided into exact distances. So is the traditional university curriculum. Everything is neat and tidy, and all courses are in little 3 x 3 blocks. Each year, universities turn out millions of graduates who, no matter how specialized, cannot do the work required in high-risk jobs. Universities educate and train people for maximum opportunities in our worldwide culture. In contrast, you are training people for *specific* job activities. Your racetrack is different because your purpose is different. Yet, a traditional curriculum gains immediate respect, because it is familiar.

- *Borrowed.* No matter how specialized your HRT mission might be, there is usually another similar one, or several, in the world. Similar, but different. Law enforcement, nuclear power plant, space travel, hospital, and flight training programs all

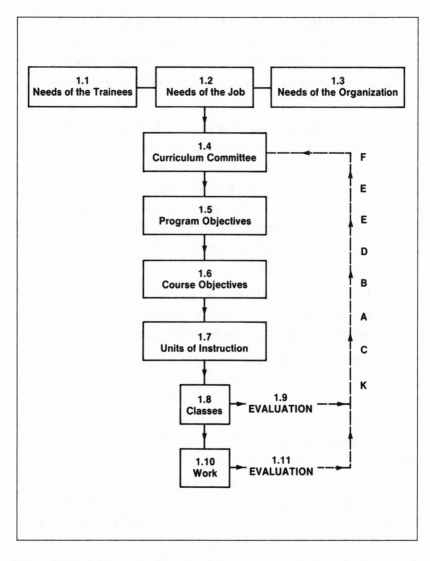

Figure 1. Model 1, curriculum development system for initial training and advancement training.

and short the track will be, versus how flat, narrow, and long. The following is a list of data requirements on the sat-techs. A core of information is always needed (e.g., previous performance in education and training, and reading levels); the requirements will vary based on the situation. The objective is to paint a word and data picture of typical trainees.

1.1.1   *Age range: young, middle-aged, or older adults.* Aging brings with it increased difficulty in accessing seldom-used numbers and facts, while youth brings immaturity and self-discipline problems.

1.1.2   *Screening test scores and reports.*

    1.1.2.1   *Reading levels.* Reading ability should determine how you package curriculum content.

    1.1.2.2   *Intelligence scores.* IQ could be equated to the horsepower of the curricules in the race.

    1.1.2.3   *Physical problems.* For example, bifocals affect simulation and may need to be fitted at the top and bottom of the lens.

1.1.3   *Past educational and training records.* Such records are one of the best predictors of success or failure. Warning: Place less faith in anything more than 3–5 years old.

    1.1.3.1   *Trends in successes or failures.* Is the trainee better in hands-on learning or theory?

    1.1.3.2   *Patterns in successes or failures.* Trainee does better away from home, fails during hunting season, etc.

1.1.4    *Work experiences.* Are trainees analytical desk-types or operations experienced?

1.1.5    *Learning and thinking styles.* Some people learn better through visual stimulation, others through auditory stimulation, others through hands-on tasks.

Add to or subtract from the list. Begin your database. Besides getting a picture of the incoming class, over time you can perform correlations to success and failure that can be fed back to the screening program. Furthermore, as other classes begin, you will have a benchmark for comparisons and can assess the need for curriculum modification. (For some unknown reason, every once in a while you will get an exceptionally bad or good class.) The data-building process can allow some field-expedient curriculum modifications (change the track a bit) to meet different needs.

The data collected in 1.1, Needs of the Trainees, will build the picture of the trainees you're dealing with and any obvious egocentrisms. Let's suppose we had twelve candidates for the sat-tech program.

- All are 32–38 years of age. (This age range is not prime, but it is certainly not over the hill for learning).

- Reading levels are average, 11.7 grade years, with no major individual deviations. (This level is about average—maybe a little high—for college graduates who have been out of school awhile).

- Intelligence scores range from 110–127, with an average of 118. (These trainees could be successful in medical school).

- No physical problems are apparent.

- All have engineering degrees and a hands-on work history. They are operations types without patterns of failure.

- The learning style of the group is essentially visual and tends to be action-oriented rather than analytical. They have an inclination toward action, which suggests that straight lectures (without interaction) should be kept to a minimum.

It is also a group of successful people; some could have ego problems in being students again. And, although their needs are important to curriculum development, the needs of the job are paramount.

## 1.2 Needs of the Job

Block 1.2, Needs of the Job, can consume most of the time and resources devoted to curriculum development. It requires—

1.2.1    Job analysis
1.2.2    Construct analysis
1.2.3    Risk assessment

A *job analysis* is the systematic dissection of the job for the purpose of determining the skills and supporting knowledge required to be successful on the job. Success includes job safety, efficiency, and effectiveness. Job analysis is conducted by interviews, observations, and use of subject-matter experts, or a combination of these methods. Job analysis has limitations:

- It merely reflects what the worker does; it cannot tell you what the worker should be doing.

- With our rate of change, a job analysis is out of date upon completion. If not continually updated, it becomes useless, even dangerous.

- A job analysis works best with hands-on workers. Its accuracy fades as job tasks move up the scale to include tasks such as monitoring and broad decision making. For example, for a manager's job, which involves making decisions in many cases with limited data, a job analysis does not reflect what goes on in the cognitive process required by the job.

The job analysis procedure was created to help decide what training was needed in America's first mechanized war, World War I. Several innovations have been made over the decades. The English have probably been the leaders in the field; even they have stopped at the work levels of dentists and pilots.

The growing need to train people in monitoring and decision-making positions is leading to the emerging field of *construct analysis*. It comes in part from Australia, and has potential for identifying the cognitive processes in monitoring and decision-making jobs. It is, however, far from a science at this writing. Nevertheless, if you are in the position of having to establish HRT for jobs that entail few hands-on tasks and many monitoring and decision-making tasks, construct analysis may help. What you do is conduct in-depth interviews with successful incumbents to identify some of the strategies they use in their work.

Another available tool is *risk assessment*. It too is an emerging science. In defining the needs of the job, risk assessment can help you determine the frequency of decision making in jobs where the central function is to evaluate, order, and structure inevitably incomplete and conflicting knowledge for the purpose of making a correct decision.

With these tools and limitations in mind, let's examine each in detail.

1.2.1 *Job analysis.* The first step of job analysis is to come up with a job description. If one is not available in the organization, in a sister organization, or in the *Dictionary of Occupational Titles* (available in most libraries), then you can build one with the aid of the personnel administrator and the group to whom the person in the position reports or will be reporting. A job description is a set of expectations. A trainer is most interested in the scope of the job, the duties and responsibilities, and the nature of the interaction with other positions.

The satellite technician description is simply stated:

> Travel in space to troubleshoot and repair weather, communications, and military satellites. Must be able to troubleshoot and replace solar battery, buffer battery, encoder, on-board computer, position-fixer transmitter, control-signal receiver, transmitter for measured data, antenna, vidicon tube TV, and control jets.

The next step is to assemble the job analysis team. Even if you are experienced in the job, don't fall prey to doing it alone. All of us are limited in our experiences. None of us have experienced everything a job could throw at us. Job analysis work is a specialization with a science of its own. A job analysis team consists of a leader, instructor, subject-matter experts (SMEs), data collectors, and computer input or clerical support. The SMEs in this case would include job incumbents, designers, electrical engineers, and experienced astronauts. Effective job analysis requires training.

The job analysis team begins their work by identifying the major blocks of the job (such as troubleshooting, replacement, testing, administration of supplies, working out of vehicle). Each major block is broken into minor blocks and tasks. Each task is broken into steps. Each step—along with a list of tools

and equipment that must be used—is broken into manipulations (skills) and what has to be known to perform the
manipulations (knowledge). For example:

X. Job: Satellite repair technician
   X.1 Major Block: Troubleshooting
     X.1.1 Minor Block: Photoelectric cells
       X.1.1.1 Task: Project life of silicon photoelectric cell.
          Tools and equipment: Photoconduc-
          tive PI—Model 100; impregnated cloth
          C–13.
       X.1.1.1.1 Steps:
         X.1.1.1.1.1 Clean contact points on cells.
           X.1.1.1.1.1.1 Know: Amount of no-freeze so-
              lution to use, that is, no more
              than two swipes of impregnated
              cloth per square centimeter.
         X.1.1.1.1.2 Measure electrical current by plac-
           ing probe A on nonmetal semicon-
           ductor and probe B on metal.
          X.1.1.1.1.2.1 Know: Interpretation of electri-
             cal current reading on
             PI—Model 100.

On it goes for perhaps hundreds of pages. Note the value
of an integrated job analysis as compared to expert opinion.
The scientific community might have said that the sat-tech,
to perform the part of the task shown, would have to know
Einstein's equation: $h\upsilon = A + \frac{1}{2}m_e v^2$. In contrast, training
covers what one *must know* to do the job; not what's nice
to know, but rather, what's most worth knowing.

There's an interesting pattern to job analysis done in this
format. Most positions will usually have between seven and
twelve major blocks (divisions of the job). The number of
tasks runs from 75 for a monitoring job to around 600 tasks

for highly skilled positions requiring technical knowledge, such as pilots, control room operators, and surgical nurses. Mechanic and technician positions tend to entail 500–600 tasks. Helpers, apprentices, and interns will normally have to perform about two-thirds of the tasks required of the position they assist. Note: If the job analysis is done correctly and identifies fewer than seven or more than twelve major blocks, management may want to review the job to determine whether duties need to be added or reduced.

All job analyses must be validated. HRT requires multiple reviews and approvals (black-ink sign-off authorization) by incumbents, supervisors, instructors, and SMEs. Some job analysis methods obtain a criticality rating of each task through the judgmental ranking of each as to difficulty, frequency, and importance. The three rankings are collapsed into a single criticality measure. Criticality ratings can be a tremendous aid to instructors during course development.

If you have many training programs for people who work in the same environment, such as a chemical plant, you can take advantage of job analysis to reduce costs. For example, you may train eight different groups of technicians, operators, and maintenance and safety personnel. You will develop eight different training programs, each with its own job analysis. To realize savings, during the initial development or the periodic revision of the job analysis, you code each skill and knowledge based on a taxonomy (a classification scheme like a library uses). You may have to develop the taxonomy for your field. It is hard work; but once done, the computer can search for all the skills and knowledges with matching classification numbers and print them out. Now you have the basis for a core training program. The core allows your other training programs to be shortened, instructors to concentrate on their specialization, employees to have more choices (rather than being committed as an operator before they really know what the job requires), and the plant to have more flexibility in selecting and placing workers on the job.

Job analysis can't do everything. To cover the portion of the job that is unobservable (few, if any, physical movements) requires a construct analysis.

1.2.2 *Construct analysis.* In work, we build, based on our experiences, a construct of how or when to perform a task. In construct analysis, to find out what constructs a particular position requires, interviews of incumbents are conducted. It is a two-sided disk. The incumbents may be wrong or right. If wrong, retraining is indicated. If right, the results may be used to determine curriculum content.

A good team to perform the interviews is an instructor and an industrial psychologist. The goal of the interviews is simple. Find out what, if anything, in the environment cues the incumbent to take actions. Identifying cues from the environment is critical. If the person is taking actions because of intuitiveness—well, besides running yourself crazy trying to figure it out—you cannot derive teachable content. Figure 2, a 5 × 4 factorial design (five blocks down and four across)

|  | People | Things | Data | Resources |
|---|---|---|---|---|
| See |  |  |  |  |
| Hear |  |  |  |  |
| Touch |  |  |  |  |
| Smell |  |  |  |  |
| Taste |  |  |  |  |

Figure 2. Environmental cues matrix.

may help interviewers ask questions that identify the environmental cues. Obviously, some of the blocks don't interact as well as others, but most do interact.

For example, "I feel the floor vibrating, then I remotely trip the pump in the room below, because it only does that when it's overloaded." "I could see the data trend starting to go downhill." "The people acted strange, guilty like, heads down, hurrying away." "I could feel the heat from the motor." "The metallic taste in my mouth told me there was a leak."

Interviews of several incumbents are required; some will not recognize, or be able to verbalize, an environmental cue. Once a set of environmental cues is identified, a validation is needed. One simple way to do the validation is to list all the cues. Accompany each with a one to five scale (unimportant to important) and have all incumbents rank each item. (Chapters 10 and 11 show how to develop scales.)

The results help you identify some teachable content or make the simple admission that some skills must be learned through OJT, which means some type of costly apprenticeship or expensive internship, neither of which guarantees learning. But there is one more tool to help out.

1.2.3 *Risk assessment.* A broad concept in high-risk organizations, risk assessment in some places means describing everything that could happen in the world generally and what the consequences would be to the operation. In others, it is more specific: "What happens if the cable on the diving bell parts?"

In HRT, risk assessment can be used to help determine the frequency and type of decision making in jobs where the central function is to evaluate, order, and structure inevitably incomplete and conflicting knowledge for the purpose of making a correct decision. An expert on decision making might say that all decisions are made under those conditions, but you know what is meant. "The jet flamed out." "The weapon was leveled." "The reactor scrammed."

Again the method is interviews, and again the team consists of an instructor and a psychologist. Certainly it can be conducted at the same time as the construct analysis. There is, however, a different focus. Here's where the shrewd instructor and the wily psychologist earn their money. They have to weed out ego-enhancing statements and get to the truth. "How often, under what conditions, without supervision, do you make critical decisions without adequate information?" The only validation is collective judgment.

The other source of information in a risk assessment is the postmortems of accidents, which often yield potentially misleading information and usually have significant holes. Most are sanitized by the organization. Interviews of survivors may yield flawed information because they may not remember what occurred due to shock or a natural self-defensiveness.

With all the problems with a risk analysis, the interviews and reviews can disclose tremendous content for simulation scenarios for training of persons operating at the higher levels of decision making, that is, making judgments in short time frames with limited options.

It all adds up. Needs of the job can be defined through job analysis, construct analysis, and risk assessment. You then know "how the job is." The next question is, "How should the job be?"

## 1.3 Needs of the Organization

The underlying motive for this block is to ensure that the training program has the input of supervisors, managers, and senior decision makers. They have to trust training, to know that the training function is responsive to their needs. This curriculum model causes an early buy-in, a sense of ownership of the program. Argument over "What's being taught?" after a program is underway can be disastrous. Although there will always be questions about content (which shows interest), this model forces the organization and the curriculum developers to make training a business, and businesslike, effort—starting up front and continuing to work together throughout the processes. The concrete training items to be addressed are:

1.3.1 Organizational values
1.3.2 Potential changes in job expectations
1.3.3 Planned changes in technology

The method of data collection is interviews. The perfect team is a member of training management (yourself) and an instructor.

1.3.1 *Organizational value.* The question is simple: How does the organization want the incumbents to behave? Which is more important, nuclear power plant safety or making megawatts? Keeping hospital beds full or providing TLC? The trick in this type of interview—which may be conducted as a group interview during a meeting—is to force hard philosophical statements on "How are we going to do business?" There is a pitfall here: Don't let it deteriorate into a session on work ethics, with management describing the ideal employee.

The question one could pose on the sat-tech program would revolve around trade-offs between conservative safety and rate of work efficiency on the satellites. The answer sets up the orientation of the curriculum, as would the statement in a military or law enforcement program, "They are expected to give up their lives for. . . ."

1.3.2 *Potential changes in job expectations.* "We're giving serious consideration to adding maintenance on deep space probes. Repair them, turn around, and send them right back out." Or, "Well, yes, I've been thinking about subcontracting that portion." Or, "Some job consolidation is in order." Find out what they are thinking. Be cautious; some of their ideas will not come to action. Such information requires monitoring.

1.3.3 *Planned changes in technology* (tools, equipment, procedures, and software). "Oh yes, we're going to trash that weapon. You guys in training didn't know that?" Such changes are must-know data.

The steps in the top tier of Model 1 are easier to present than to perform. The task is painstaking, costly, and time-consuming, and it requires handling massive quantities of data. At the completion, however, you will have defined the job, identified characteristics of the trainees, and involved the organization in rounding out the job. All data are catalogued and validated. Now you have to decide what's there that you don't need, which brings us to the next block.

## 1.4 Curriculum Committee

Deciding what's most worth knowing is the key. The research activities undertaken in blocks 1.1–1.3 will have yielded a massive amount of data about the job and how it will evolve in the near future. The role of the curriculum committee is to decide what is in the data that is not worth knowing and what should be emphasized. The results of the committee's work are program objectives. The make-up of the committee is crucial.

- *Curriculum committee manager* who is a supervisor or manager from the training staff. Beyond all the administrative headaches of setting the meetings, the manager's job is to bring about consensus among the committee members on what goes out and on program objectives.

- *Training supervisor* under whose area the training will be accomplished. The supervisor has many roles in the meeting—advisor, interpreter, refiner—but the main role is predicting the capability of the training group in accomplishing the programs. The supervisor must possess a realistic view of what can be done within the operating constraints of time, staff, budgets, and space.

- *Instructor(s)* who will be conducting the training. Their roles are multiple. In addition to helping weed down the job analysis, they must offer creative ways to divide the racetrack into courses and package the courses. Estimating time required for a course and how things could be taught (lab, simulator, and the like) are critical elements of their input.

- *Supervisor* to whom those completing the program shall report. This person is the most vital link from the training staff to the organization. This person must help build the program and has to give and take in light of constraints. The involvement of the supervisor is critical to the trust factor of training and future support of a training schedule.

- *Incumbent(s)* who work daily in the field in which the training is to be done. Their role is to bring reality to the data. "That's not hard. Make damn sure they know how to do this. Everyone always forgets. . . ."

- *Recorder* who will keep accurate minutes. Preserving a written document that correctly reflects what occurred is crucial. Internal and external auditors may pore over the minutes on a regular basis. In case of an accident, the holes in the sleeves get tight.

Curriculum committees exist for each curriculum. These are standing committees that not only meet for initial development but continue to meet to review, evaluate, provide feedback, and approve curriculum changes.

An excellent way to begin a meeting is with a nuts-and-bolts discussion of the needs of the trainees, block 1.1. Next is a presentation of projected changes in the job or technology and the views of senior management based on the work performed for block 1.3. Getting those items firmly established in peoples' minds is useful before reviewing the job analysis conducted for block 1.2.

With printouts for everyone, the committee does a line-by-line walk-down of the job analysis. It is tedious and tough work. Remember, the goal is to take things out. On occasion there will be additions. Mostly, it's a reality screen: "Do we really have to teach engineers about . . .?" "It is ridiculous to waste time on. . . ." "This area could be collapsed into a review. . . ." "Here's the big one." Whittling the job analysis down is a difficult task, and arguments will occur. The curriculum committee manager must maintain control and achieve consensus.

## 1.5 Program Objectives

Once the committee has removed from the job analysis the items that are nice to know or trainees already know, it is time to generate program objectives. The racetrack is divided into segments, with the program objectives identifying the courses on the track. Do not confuse program objectives with measurable learning objectives; those come later from the instructors. Let's look at the program objectives for our example, the sat-tech training program:

- Basic Electronics and Electricity
- Instruments and Controls
- Measuring Devices
- Physical Properties
- Test Instruments and Calibration
- Print Reading
- Troubleshooting
- Space Living
- Out-of-Vehicle Safety
- Administrative Procedures
- Radiation Detection and Dosimetry
- Millimeter Wave Radar

The program objectives identify broad training areas, often corresponding to (but not limited to) the major blocks identified in the job analysis.

Although perhaps not the role of the curriculum committee, there is one additional administrative task to be accomplished: establishing a tracking mechanism that will tie each task to a program objective. Building the tracking system so it can follow the tasks into each course and down to each unit of instruction will streamline course updates later.

## 1.6 Course Objectives

The job is now for the instructional staff and whatever support staff might exist to establish course objectives and specifications. You want course objectives to be measurable and stated in terms of performance. For example—

At the completion of the space-living course, the successful completers will be competent to take care of themselves for extended periods of time in space.

Specifically, the completers will—

- plan and prepare meals
- maintain sanitation standards
- maintain physical condition
- conduct in-space housekeeping chores
- design a recreation and relaxation program

Arriving at general course objectives is a mental process with few guidelines or rules. No computer program can do this successfully. The instructors, support personnel, and supervisors pull out similar content from the job analysis and group it into teachable blocks, again tying each task (by a trackable number) to the appropriate course objective.

Now is the time—when establishing course objectives for the various courses on the track—to sequence the courses. The most common sequence is from simple to complex. Do the reviews, set the basic courses, and build from there to more difficult content.

Some specifications can be added to course objectives based on the job task analysis:

> Plan and prepare meals
> *Knowledge*: Basic nutrition and food prep-
> aration routine
> *Skills*: Operation of model 12–K1 stove,
> model 12–K2 food storage unit, and 12–
> K3 compactor; updating of food inventory
> program 6 Delta

Speculation on how the course is to be taught and estimated course length should be included:

> *Training approach*:
> Lecture or computer-based training on
> nutrition; simulation on operation of

kitchen; part-task simulation on inventory
program
*Estimated length*: 4–6 hours

This course can now be developed into teachable content.
Whenever possible, this work should be done by the people
who will do the teaching. It ensures they trust the content.
If the development has to be done out-of-house or through
outright purchase from a vendor, give the instructor(s) revision
or approval rights. Once instructors close the door to the
simulator, lab, shop, classroom, they will do what they believe
is correct. If teaching content is shoved down their throats,
they will do it, but then they will lay it aside and say, "Now
let me tell you what you really need to know." Telling isn't
teaching, and you will have wasted money on purchasing the
course. Furthermore, remember, there is some reason if the
instructor lacks faith in the material. It may be a good reason.

## 1.7 Units of Instruction
A unit of instruction is the actual teaching and learning
material used in a course by the instructor and the trainees,
one document for both. In HRT, secrets as to what is to be
learned are not kept from the students, and guessing games
on what is most important to learn and what competencies
will be tested should never be played. Remember, the objective
is learning. Always let them know what is important to learn.
Stating the competencies to be tested does not mean receiving
the test questions beforehand.

The unit of instruction format presented in this book is
more than a hybrid lesson plan, although it does contain
familiar parts. This format is based on the best current
knowledge of structuring learning for the adult mind and has
proven itself in over six years of use in HRT.

There is a training management function that needs to take place after an instructor and—if you are lucky—a technical writer have drafted a unit of instruction. The draft is circulated to the using group (supervisors of the group for whom the trainees will work) for review of learning objectives, technical information, references, and manner of instruction. The reviews (which must be kept timely by training management) are returned to the instructor for resolution of comments. Following the usual rewrites, all involved give written authorization by signing off on the cover sheet of the unit of instruction: the instructor, the training manager, the training supervisor, and the work group supervisor. The reviews are another way to have the user group be owners of the courses, and if an internship or job facility training space is required, the reviews help gain commitment to support the course. The reviews also mean something to the trainees, who will see the supervisor's name on the units of instruction and will know their boss approved the content.

The format elements for a unit of instruction include:

1.7.1 *Title page.* Course title, number, length, revision number, date of last revision, identification numbers of task(s) covered, and sign-off lines.

1.7.2 *Objectives page.* Terminal objectives of the course and enabling objectives. All are written to include conditions under which the learner is to demonstrate competence and passing or failing scores. When possible (which is most of the time), each objective should carry the identification numbers of the task(s) it covers.

1.7.3 *Reference page.* All references used to develop the unit, including procedures, standards, drawings, books, articles, and interviews with experts must be listed. Attention to latest revision of references must be made. ANSI–3.5 is not good enough; ANSI–3.5 with revision number followed by month and year is correct. Any difficult-to-find material should have its physical location noted.

1.7.4 *Instructional materials and equipment page.* Everything—tools, tapes, drawings, overheads, etc.—must be listed to aid in instructor efficiency.

1.7.5 *Information sheets* (the text of the course). Each objective is explained with examples. Only the must-know information is included. It is *not* a script for the instructor; it is information that presents the content that the trainee is to learn. Trainees use it as their textbook; the instructor lectures from it but is not limited by the content. The instructor must cover what is there but can add more.

1.7.6 *Assignment sheets.* Predetermined pencil-and-paper exercises on application of formulas, practice creating line drawings of a system, and the like.

1.7.7 *Job sheets.* Predetermined laboratory or shop hands-on experiments or manipulations (e.g., given a BX32, troubleshoot the current flow; disassemble the jet pump). Each job sheet is a learning, practice device that provides step-by-step directions. It spreads the instructor "thicker" in the application stage.

1.7.8 *Handout sheets.* You can save time and errors during class by packaging all handouts, drawings, plans, copies of photographs, and hard copies of all overhead transparencies. Sets of handouts are a great time saver in class for both the instructor and the trainees, and they ensure that everyone has the same information.

Consider the simple structural lines of the first eight parts of a unit of instruction and their contribution to efficiency and effective learning and teaching. Everyone knows what is expected from them because of the objectives page. The information sheets give the whys, thus making what is learned transferable to other situations. The assignment and job sheets cause the trainees to apply the information (the key to learning and retention) in a practice, no-threat situation. All handouts are prepackaged. Then there is the last section, which is kept under lock and key with limited access: performance evaluation.

1.7.9 *Performance evaluation.* In the unit of instruction format, evaluation is an extrapolation from the learning objectives. Face validity is achieved by matching the test item to the objective, whether it is simple—"List four parts of a. . . ."—or difficult—"Under accident conditions bring the plant into a stable condition."

Performance evaluations come in whatever form is needed: pencil and paper, hands-on, simulation, interview, or a combination. Sometimes you may be tempted not to have pencil-and-paper tests. But, remember the advantages they offer. Besides the content, you can also test reading, comprehension, and direction-following abilities. About 30 percent of our population has a reading problem of one type or another, which is a concern to you as a trainer.

## 1.8 through 1.11 Feedback Loops

Part 3 of this book is devoted to evaluation. It presents in-depth discussion on evaluation and the feedback loops from classes and work performance. Briefly, feedback loops test the learning (and difficulties) of trainees in the course and—the true test of all training—whether the learning was applied on the job. If not, why? Wrong material? Not retained? Supervisor did not carry through?

When learning is not applied or the rate of application falls over time, something has to be done. One way is through management attention. Another is to use Model 2, the system for developing curriculums for retraining and continuous training.

## Model for Retraining and Continuing Training

The philosophy of Model 2 is different. There is no such occurrence as "trained." Training is a life-spanning activity; it is never finished.

The lessons of not doing as trained or not keeping up are frequent in our history. Take the story of Jack Phillips, "Sparks," the radioman on the *Titanic*. Radios were the high-tech product in 1912. Surely, anyone who could use one must know all about the things. Jack didn't know the international distress code had been changed to S.O.S., so he tapped the old one while 2,228 people panicked; 1,523 died. In another example, the chain of events that led up to the Three Mile Island Unit 2 accident had happened earlier at another reactor. Had the operators known the sequences and understood the odd readings, they would not have kept shutting off the automatic safety systems.

Technical training is not all that is needed. In commercial aviation, the "old corps" approach that the captain knows everything and the first officer and navigators will only "speak when spoken to" has tremendous costs. Although there are humorous cases—landing not only on the wrong runway, but at the wrong airport—too often, the result is death. Phony status and arrogance cost; cockpit management and assertiveness training are needed.

Model 2 (figure 3) has four subparts on the top tier: 2.1, Demands of Technology; 2.2, Demands of Work; 2.3, Demands of Personnel; and 2.4, Demands of Organization. The challenge is to establish a monitoring, tracking, and validation system (blocks 2.5 through 2.7) that is manageable and doesn't bury the instructors under printouts. Blocks 2.8 through 2.15 correspond to those explained for Model 1.

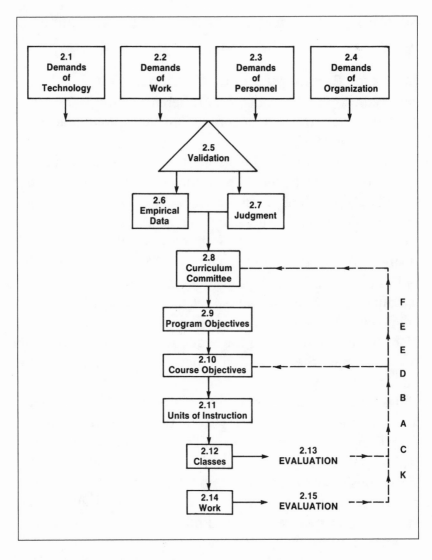

Figure 3. Model 2, curriculum development system for retraining and continuing training.

## 2.1 Demands of Technology

Monitoring is required to discover changes in equipment and uncover existing technology that doesn't work as it should.

Sources vary from organization to organization. On the broad scale, there are usually professional journals; technical reports from industry, service, or government agencies; and research reports from universities, test laboratories, and private institutions. On the local scene, there are long-term planning groups as well as purchasing groups whose members know exactly what changes are coming immediately. Unsatisfactory equipment reports and audits of work orders provide information on continuing problems with hardware and software.

## 2.2 Demands of Work

Jobs evolve. In a startup operation, changes in job responsibilities come fast and furious. In established situations, job changes occur at a slower rate. A new bargaining-unit contract can result in changes in job activities. The growing fields of leasing, external maintenance contracts, and specialized vendors can change a job a technician is doing from troubleshooting and repair to parts changing and inspection. New written work procedures, work package systems, auditors' reports, and accident reports add to immense numbers of work changes that affect training.

## 2.3 Demands of Personnel

In a highly transient work group (such as a military station) or where the same team rarely works together (such as cockpit crews and attendants in commercial aviation), there is a high demand for retraining. The same need can exist in any work force that suddenly sees a high turnover rate or brings in significant numbers of so-called qualified people for a major outage at a plant. There are lessons that can be learned from permanent personnel about working with a mobile, rapidly changing work force to make up for transients' deficiencies in on-site or hardware-specific knowledge. This principle also holds true for temporary personnel or workers brought in temporarily from other installations to cover for regular employees during a period of rampant illness or emergencies.

## 2.4 Demands of Organization

The demands an organization places on employees change. Sometimes the changes are radical and rapid. A new technology is introduced. New hardware arrives, and new procedures are implemented. Or, perhaps the entire work force is moved to a new location. Other times, the changes occur more slowly. Policies and procedures are always being modified. These minor changes can accumulate into significant differences in how people perform their work. Changes, fast or slow, threaten the validity of the curriculum. Training must never be the last to know. Training must be the first to know when the demands placed on employees change. To keep ahead with the curriculum requires monitoring.

## Curriculum Data and Tracking System

Blocks 2.1 through 2.4 can use the same data collection and tracking system. The curriculum data tracking and validation system shown in figure 4 fulfills the tracking requirements and accomplishes the work of block 2.5, Validation, through 2.6, Empirical Data, or 2.7, Judgment. There are three main steps in the system.

1. *Identify data sources.* Supplement paper sources by building routine communication links with design engineers (What may change the simulator?), purchasing personnel, senior decision makers, and line personnel. Line people, those in the trenches, usually have weekly or daily briefings or meetings. A training staff member should attend some or all of those meetings to obtain information for Model 2. The individual (preferably an instructor who has responsibility for

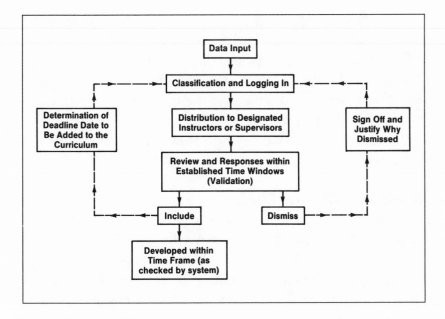

Figure 4. System for tracking and validating curriculum data.

retraining and continuing training) needs to fully understand Model 2 and how to properly phrase the asking of the right questions and should have a sense of timing.

2. *Formalize data sources.* Chapter 4, Developing Procedures, and chapter 8, Utilizing Procedures, describe the process in detail. The concept is that approved procedures can make reporting information to the training division a part of other people's work. A supervisory touch is needed to make sure incumbents understand the need to accurately report information.

3. *Build a tracking system.* Depending on the magnitude of the data, the system can be pencil and paper or tracked by computer. It is amazing how much can be managed with a pencil-and-paper system. Of course, a microcomputer can take the drudgery out of the process.

Validation is accomplished by the instructor during the development phase. The instructor does so (with supervision) through empirical data (scientific, measurable data) or the judgment of subject-matter experts. Retain the validation documentation. Besides meeting the curriculum committee's need to review the proof, it is useful for dealing with auditors and building a methodology file (How did we prove this the last time?).

## Curriculum Change Strategy

This monitoring capability, which is built into Model 2, is ideal to drive curriculum revisions for initial training and advancement training covered by Model 1. For example, using Model 1, you develop an initial curriculum for in-space satellite repair technicians. To keep the sat-techs on their toes (retraining) and up to date (continuing training), you use Model 2. These changes must be introduced to Model 1 to see if changes are required in the initial curriculum. It is an excellent and economical change device that ensures the freshness of the initial curriculum.

It works the same way for the advancement curriculum. These programs are usually taught less frequently and have a higher potential of being stale (instructors see the material less frequently, and trainees critique the material less often). New material from Model 2 can drive changes in advancement training. Recall the earlier emphasis on tracking the job task through course objectives and unit of instruction objectives. Now you have the payoff. New material that has been identified and tagged to a job task can easily be traced to a specific objective in one or several units of instruction. A reliable tracking system simplifies updating and ensures that all changes are made.

A curriculum is the job-related training experiences the trainees move through in preparation for the future. Curriculum development for a particular job is the process of identifying and validating what is most worth knowing from the world of what possibly could be taught. Curriculum development of initial training, retraining, continuing training, and advancement training is managed by the use of curriculum models. The two models presented here interact for updating existing curriculums. The models ensure the participation of line, senior, and expert personnel. Their involvement, in turn, contributes to training programs being accepted and supported.

# 3
# Developing Staff

The pipes in the plumber's home leak. The mechanic's car never receives preventive maintenance. The police officer's son. . . . On it goes. There is time for everyone else, but not for ourselves—an easy trap. Successful trainers tend to be "helping people" by nature. People who put aside their own needs to fulfill the needs of others. Watch out. Helping is one thing, but being a people-pleaser, never able to say no, is costly. Canceling training for the training staff, freeing them to conduct other training, cheats the staff and eventually the work groups who deserve the best possible training. There is a way out.

This chapter presents ways to excel at staff development in an efficient, effective, and superior manner. Because your trainers are also adult learners, the ways presented here can be transferred to solve training problems in work groups. But first you must understand the concept of leadership, the reality of leadership in staff development and self-development, and how to design staff development.

## Concept of Leadership

| LEADER | SHIP |
|--------|------|
| ↓ | ↓ |
| AHEAD | OTHERS |

The original word came from the swashbuckling days of wooden-masted armadas. A leadership would be sent ahead just over the horizon of the ocean where the mast could still be seen. The job of the leadership was to monitor weather, watch for landfall, and be on the lookout for shoals and enemy fleets. The rest of the armada would watch the mast of the leadership. As it changed course, they too, the followships, would alter course to match the leadership.

There were three problems with the armada leadership. If it stayed too close to the rest of the armada, it could not provide direction on the future course any better than other ships. Arguments occurred and confusion resulted. If it went too far over the horizon, its mast could not be seen, and it provided no direction to the followships. Again, confusion and lack of a clear direction to the future occurred. The third problem arose when the followships did not trust the ability of the leadership to plot the future course.

What might have caused a lack of trust? The leadership may not have taken the time to develop trust through personal interaction and communication and by proving to the group that the organization's mission and the staff's welfare were kept uppermost in mind. The leadership, having failed to plot a good course across troughs and swells, may not have come back to admit its mistake and take the blame for rough sailing. The leadership may not have learned from mistakes or perhaps never knew how to plot a course; it just kept on going, "plotting" along, and, finally, alone.

The right to lead must be earned, not at the expense of followers but with their help, input, and expertise. Some may have sailed the waters before, or be excellent at reading the weather and the water (the trends of the future). Most certainly, they should best know the capabilities of their own ships to withstand the course to the future.

Followships are difficult to gain. They have been led off course too often and suffered the consequences. They have seen the leadership add sail, skirt the storm, and leave them to fight their own way through. Or, they have worked hard to keep up with the leadership, only to find a party was going on aboard the leadership while they were doing all the work.

A followship is gained by being technically competent to plot a course, communicating the mission and the whys, and standing up for the followship. Dedication to the mission and to the people who have to carry it out are not mutually exclusive activities. Picking one over the other results in failure. Good leaders hold the organization and the people up high. Neither takes precedence over the other.

The fateful lesson of leadership is simple: like trust, once lost it can never be regained.

## Leadership in Staff Development

The training staff, like you, did not plan to be in training. None of you made a conscious career decision at seventeen to become a trainer. Trainers are different from lawyers, health professionals, teachers—people who selected a career and pursued the educational track of entry into the career. Trainers are in their jobs because of coincidence and chance. Training is, for most, a second career. Some may not even consider it a career, just a way station, a place to get a ticket punched and move on, a means to get off shift work, a safer environment in which to wait out retirement. Why your staff members are there probably doesn't matter. You have them, and you have the responsibility to provide leadership to these people with diverse backgrounds. A blessing and a curse come with the territory.

The blessing is that staff members' diverse backgrounds bring the technical expertise required for instruction and a rich field of experiences for problem solving. The curse is that your trainers undoubtably do not have a common mentality, which causes two problems:

- You can't start in the middle and expect your communications to be received. In the past, when you communicated with a group who had the same background and experiences you had, you could be an efficient communicator. A foundation of concepts was shared by all. Those shared concepts do not exist in a training staff until you develop them.

- Because of their diverse backgrounds, your training staff members have a predisposition about, an already existing image of, a leader. Each background brings a different view, a learned view, of what leaders should look like and how leaders should behave. You can't earn their followership and provide leadership into the future until some commonalities in viewpoints—trust factors—are developed.

Staff development is the way to pull the group together and obtain a common mentality of training. In the process, a followership is built and leadership becomes viable for developing a course of action for the future. It is not a simple task. Most views of leadership were formed early in the work life of each staff member. Whatever adults learn first, they hold onto the longest; their diverse views can be very strongly held. Figure 5 is a simple diagram of how jobs increasingly influence our lives.

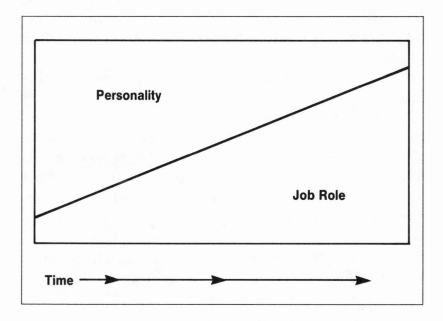

Figure 5. Role-personality displacement model.

For decades, researchers of the whys, whats, and hows of formal work organizations have referred to incumbents as actors, actors with a role to fulfill in the formal organization. The actors' roles are defined by the formal expectations in a job description and the informal expectations presented by the unwritten values of the organization. Over time, one's personality is displaced by the role of the job. The amount of time varies from organization to organization. The Marine Corps does a reasonably thorough job of basic military training at Parris Island in eight to ten weeks, and the organization, after recruit training, reinforces the role. In contrast, in a laissez-faire organization, like a university, professors and administrators may take as long as five years to begin acting like stereotyped professors and deans.

The displacement of your personality by a role is not limited to a paying job. It occurs when you leave home, get married, become a parent, get a divorce, whatever. Personality displacement, per se, is not bad. Yet few of us like the idea of tinkering around with someone's mind.

Unfortunately, staff development means personality displacement. Fortunately, the participants, as training staff members, are essentially volunteers. They participate freely, and, even in the most authoritarian organizations, have choices. Besides, your staff is developing right now, with or without your direction. The personality displacement required to develop as a trainer is not the equivalent of a brain transplant. The drive in staff development of trainers is not to make everyone think, look, and act alike; that would be counterproductive. Innovation—the ability to read the need to alter and set a new course—must be retained. Your goals for your staff members should be to—

- Goal 1: Learn core concepts of training
- Goal 2: Learn how to effectively and efficiently apply their unique expertise in the training environment
- Goal 3: Learn the limitations and capabilities of their training function
- Goal 4: Develop the leadership and followship skills needed to set, readjust, and change the course into the future

Staff development is training and more. Even though creativity cannot be taught—training can't add that extra brain cell—a program can present methods for innovation, give permission to be innovative, and suggest ways of implementing innovation. Everyone has a good idea. Ideas just need to be developed, like leadership and followship.

Training environments, because of the diversity of staff expertise, make each member at once a leader in his or her area and a follower in other areas. That attitude has to be developed. The place to begin is with your own development. Remember, you're an adult learner, too.

## Self-Development

You have already begun learning the core concepts of training like the curriculum models in chapter 2. The models are ideal for developing training for staff. You are in the same position as the supervisor of the work groups for whom you do HRT. You need to orchestrate the completion of block 1.3, Needs of the Organization (What should the incumbents do?), in Model 1, and you need to have input on blocks 2.1 through 2.4 in Model 2, the demands of technology, work, personnel, and organization. Those demands require leadership acts, and leadership in training requires development.

Leadership of a multidisciplined training staff requires strategies that differ from those required for leadership of a group of like professionals. The style that appeals to operations and line-background people will turn off specialists, technicians, and professionals who know you can't order success. The style that appeals to researchers, job and task analysts, programmers, and others whose approach is let's study it some more will turn off those who know that a decision has to be made so work can be done, that vacillating on a decision is deadly.

Law Number One: *Leadership styles are not transferable.* Followship in an R&D unit cannot be developed with a line orientation. The federal government cannot be run like a business; the system is not rational, it's political. A business cannot be run like an army, because (unlike in the army) the people are free to leave. Success as a leader in one field will not make you a success in another, different, foreign field—like HRT. The transfer of your previously successful style will come closer to making you a failure. The purpose of leadership, setting the direction for the future, does not change. But there are other ways to do it, another style, a style you have to develop. The development begins with self-appraisal, looking at your self-concept.

The power to see ourselves is a true power. It is not a gift; it must be learned. Seeing ourselves in reality—not as we imagine others see us—is hard work. There is an ancient sociological idea called the Looking Glass Theory, "What I imagine others think of me." It leads to mentally rehearsing an interaction and receiving feedback before the event occurs. Then, because we already know the outcome (through our rehearsal), we tend to ignore or downplay the reality of what does happen and declare the event a success. Perhaps this explanation overstates the Looking Glass Theory, because few of us are so dogmatic as to totally deny reality. Yet, we are "looking glass" enough to rationalize a bit of success out of our imagery. How many of us have said at one time or another, "They didn't understand me because they're operations types, pencil pushers, academicians, bean counters, researchers, programmers. . .? It's their fault, not mine."

We will change and develop when we examine ourselves and others critically enough. Most of us do, but we can do it better if we get rid of our filters. What we perceive is influenced by how we see ourselves. Our thinking, internalized action, is based on our convictions. Instructors will teach as they were taught, even though they will be the first to admit their instructors were not very good. There's something wrong here.

Your past experiences have taught you to manage the known and predictable in your previous work. They have not taught you how to manage situations that are yet to occur, like you will face in HRT. If you've already faced several unpredicted situations, how much of the results did you imagine? If the results were bad, reality no doubt hit you in the face like a mugger with a sharpened chain, and you surely had a significant emotional experience. If you haven't faced a situation like that yet, wait awhile. There are plenty of "life's little levelers" out there and big levelers too that may cost lives.

You don't have to wait for the leveler. Get ahead of it. You can increase your reading of reality. We all can in HRT, and it is our responsibility. We must get better at setting the leadership in the right direction for the future. Sometimes we read reality inefficiently and perhaps not as a conscious act, unless it jumps on us. More frequently, we have to force ourselves to read reality. Reality testing is the phrase.

Consider this scenario. You are having a phone conversation with an old friend you haven't communicated with in five years. "Changed much?" your friend asks. You respond that you are still the same. You just lied, but unintentionally. For the past five years, you have been redefining your view of the world. Based on your redefinition, you have been changing your constructs of work, love, family, money, status, and everything that is important to you. Our constructs change as we interpret the events around us. Each separate construct is the repository of what has been learned.

To provide leadership and followship requires relearning faster. There is, however, a natural resistance to this. But, remember, committing to relearning better does not mean you are currently in the wrong. It means you want to get better at reading reality, to cut down on your denial of reality. It is difficult. Someone who has been aggressive for years cannot suddenly become, without difficulty, insightful and cooperative. Nor may that even be required.

All that is required is a commitment to leadership growth, maturity. No matter how long we lead and follow, we are still maturing. Leadership growth is a lifelong process that requires constant reality testing, daily, hourly, even minute by minute. A formalized reality testing program is a way of doing more (with greater accuracy) of what we already do for survival (except better). Figure 6 presents the reality testing of a construct, using the example of the construct of leadership. The process is not meant to make a leader a slave to the followship. The process is meant to cause growth so that a course to be followed can be achieved in a competent manner.

*Step 1.* The first step in leadership growth can be cynically referred to as the "falling out of love with self" step. It is also the hardest because we naturally resist admitting that we filter our perceptions, are unrealistic, have disparities in our self-concept, and are fuzzy overall in our self-appraisal.

The more uncomfortable this step makes you feel, the more you need the process. By definition, a construct has evolved from learning pulled from your experiences. It is an organized pattern of attitudes, habits, knowledge, and drives that have proven successful for you. It's threatening to say, "I'm not good enough; I have been kidding myself; I'm a phony."

You don't have to say those things. You do, however, have to admit that there are things you don't know. You can become a better, more competent leader. The way to do it is through reality testing

*Step 2.* In the second step, leadership growth requires self-examination. The purpose is to lay the groundwork for insight. Genuine glimpses of self are reached, and the growth is begun

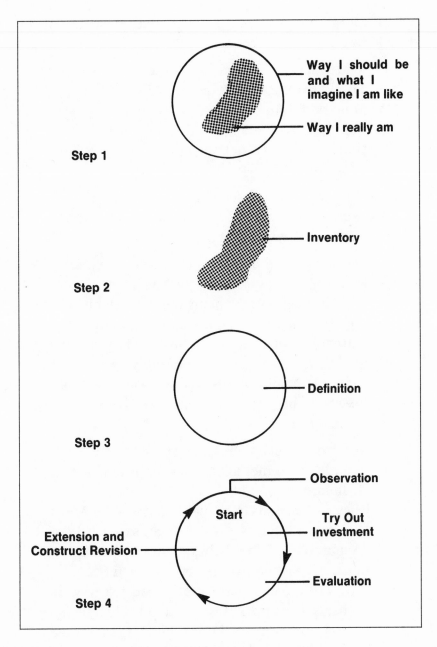

Figure 6. Leadership growth steps.

by an inventory. One way to take that inventory is by questioning self:

Q: Where have I learned how to lead? Where did I build my construct?

A: Military training; working in operations; patrolling the street; being a professor; in the space shuttle program (but I was a pilot before); as head floor nurse. . . .

Q: Who were my followers?

A: Army engineers; licensed operators; my partner; students; crew; RNs. . . .

Q: What traits and behaviors worked for me?

A: Knowing the equipment; speaking loudly; keeping my shoes shined; being the most technically qualified and knowing the plant; supporting my partner in dangerous situations and knowing the law; being firm, fair, and friendly; possessing technical qualifications, giving clear directions, knowing the procedures; always checking on them, teaching them. . . .

Q: What made people respect me? trust me? have confidence in me? (This question is a hard one. Be honest.)

A: They had to, I was in charge, and it was the Army; I knew my business in the plant, saved it from a scram once, I could always answer their questions; bravery on the streets, I got a medal; uh, I knew the course, also I told good jokes; well, probably because I was a test pilot before the shuttle, and everyone knows; I kept them in line on the floors, made them work hard. . . .

There is another way, but it really hurts. Vary it any way you want; it lets you know what others think. Call your training staff together, and include your peers. Tell them you're reassessing your management style. Give them blank pieces of paper. Assure them that you will never see their handwriting, that their comments will go directly to a confidential clerk. Then ask them to write down three things they like about you and three things they don't like about you. Have the clerk collect, type, and destroy the originals. Talk about an eye-opener. You will also find out if they trust you.

*Step 3.* The third step is never finished. It is a dual process of your definition of the leadership construct needed and the viewpoints of the followship. Your first action is to analyze the backgrounds and expertise of the staff. For example, suppose you have seventeen people: eleven are instructors, with seven of the eleven coming from other sites and none of the eleven instructors having college degrees; the remaining six are from the educational sector and include a test and measurements specialist with a Ph.D., one curriculum specialist with a master's degree, and four educational technologists (with B.S. degrees) for programming the part-task simulator. This group is diverse but falls into two distinct categories of backgrounds.

Interview them one by one: "What are your expectations? Where should we be going? How shall we get there?" If you can't interview, have another group meeting. The charge is simple. "If you took over my job tomorrow, what are the first three things you would do?" Have the rules of confidentiality as before. Besides their definitions, you will also pick up personnel issues that need addressing.

Another activity to be accomplished is a candid conversation with the person to whom you report for feedback. The entire goal is to define the construct, the core leadership acts that will get the followships to change course when the leadership strikes out into the future.

*Step 4.* The last step is to test your modified construct in action. You make an observation, invest time in trying out a new leadership act, and evaluate the results, and if it's successful, you have enlarged your construct. Evaluation is the key action. How do you know if it really (in reality) worked?

Monitor the environment. You have five senses and "pay attention" channels in your brain. Stretch those channels by observing everything around you, with your senses. Get the filters off. But, keep in mind, even though you will never make everyone happy, you do need to have a consensus of the followship before they will follow you; otherwise, sabotage will wreck the trek into the future.

Here is a list to build from and ask questions about:

- *Immediate verbal and nonverbal reactions*: Cries; moans; throwing things; frowns; smiles; passive, arms crossed, looking away; arms open, looking at you; absenteeism; late arrival; early leaving

- *Intermediate reactions*: Statements made voluntarily or elicited, such as "good," "bad," "I don't care"; work started, not started; asking you for advice; gossip, what the grapevine says; meetings called on their own to get the project moving or to plot your overthrow; people bidding out, quitting, or asking for transfers (sometimes that has to happen to a few people)

- *Long-term test*: Was the project completed successfully and what did it cost?

Building your leadership construct is never over because things are always changing. Constant monitoring is required.

What was right today may not be right tomorrow. Live, observe, try out, and learn. Now let's scope out how to develop your staff.

## Designing Staff Development

Start by developing a staff matrix (figure 7 is an example). Across the top are groupings of jobs. Down the side are core concepts and areas of application of expertise; the list could extend to hundreds of skills.

Recall the four staff development goals given earlier in this chapter. The basic design of the staff matrix helps you with the first two goals—helping staff members learn core concepts of training and how to apply individual expertise in the training environment. Let's look at the third goal, for the staff to learn the limitations and capabilities of their functional area. There are three reasons behind this goal. The first is that you don't want a staff member overcommitting. The credibility of training, like leadership, can be lost on one massive failure or on an accumulation of several smaller failures. Don't let the people-pleasers, those who can't say no, ruin a training function. Don't allow them to sit across the table during a curriculum meeting and shake their heads yes to every request, demand, and suggestion. That kind of acquiescence will kill a program and eventually people.

The second reason is the need for training staff members to know how much rough water they can take as a followship. Don't let them overcommit to you as the leadership.

The third reason is the other side of the disk. You don't want training services, facilities, simulators, software, or computers underutilized. Herein rests the key to productivity—more learning for each dollar invested. The key is innovation. Walk into an empty classroom and ask, What can be done to increase learning in a lecture in this room? Wander

| | Instructors | Curriculum Developers | Software Developers | Hardware Maintenance | Job and Task Specialists | Supervisors | Administrators |
|---|---|---|---|---|---|---|---|
| Purpose of Training | R | R | R | R | R | R | R |
| Concept of Curriculum | R | R | S | * | R | R | * |
| Concept of Adult Learning | R | R | R | * | R | R | * |
| Concept of Job Analysis | R | R | R | * | R | R | * |
| Concept of Evaluation | R | R | R | * | S | R | * |
| Purpose of Simulation | R | R | R | * | R | R | * |
| Instructional Practice | R | S | R | * | * | R | * |
| Unit of Instruction Development | R | S | S | * | S | R | R |
| Simulator Scenario Development | R | S | R | * | * | R | * |
| Test Security | R | R | R | R | R | R | R |

R = Required    S = Suggested    * = Not Needed

Figure 7. Example of a staff development matrix.

over to the simulator; go past the CBT (computer-based training) room; go into the lab, the shop; go out to the firing range, the field simulation area; go into the plant, out into the wards, onto the street, into the maintenance hangars. What can be done to increase learning in all those training areas and on-the-job activities?

Getting more learning for each dollar invested does not mean making training longer, harder, or shorter. If a lecture is the wrong way to deliver a specific learning task, making it longer won't help. How can the quality of learning be increased, leading to longer retention and job application? How can that question be made a part of the thinking of the training staff as they go about their daily work? What efficiencies lie just beyond their current view of the world?

To suggest that something deliberate can be done to make people have new ideas is questionable. To suggest that people can be developed to look for new information or to look at old information in a new way is realistic. Figure 8 is a matrix for developing innovation in training.

Figure 8 is not a model of thinking. It is a model to use in classifying staff members and deciding on some of their development needs. Thinking is presented in two dimensions; levels and maturity. Each is divided into three parts:

*Thinking Levels:*
1. Recall: Knowing something and being able to access it
2. Relate: Tying together those things known
3. Create: Taking what's tied together and making something new

*Thinking Maturity:*
a. Record: Establishing a memory of solutions
b. Linear: Extrapolating from a memory of solutions
c. Divergent: Expanded multilevel (even circular perhaps) thinking patterns that arrive at nontraditional and unique solutions

| | | | THINKING LEVELS | | |
|---|---|---|---|---|---|
| | | | 1<br>Recall | 2<br>Relate | 3<br>Create |
| **THINKING MATURITY** | a | Record | 1a | 2a | 3a |
| | b | Linear | 1b | 2b | 3b |
| | c | Divergent | 1c | 2c | 3c |

Figure 8.  Innovation development matrix.

A new staff member, inexperienced in training, begins in cell 1a. Assume the person is an instructor who requires a basic train-the-trainer course on how to give a lecture, answer a question, use the video machine, and ask a question. In the process of training, the instructor-to-be learns the basics (to recall when needed) and records some pat solutions (e.g., here's what you do when a trainee wants to help you teach and doesn't know anything).

Usually, training programs for training staff stop at cell 1a. Then, by experience or osmosis in some way, the staff member works through 1b and 2a and gets to cell 2b. A staff member in 2b has a repertoire of straight, linear solutions (try solution x, then y, then z) to problems encountered, as one training concept is related to another and practiced. Most trainers (not all) can get only as far as cell 2b on their own experiences. Too often, they must spend a long time—years—filled with trial and error, frustration, resistance, and, finally, resignation to the system. The challenge for training management is to provide quality training for cell 1a, to help the staff to get to cell 2b as rapidly and prudently as possible, and then to help people stretch into creativity and divergency.

Productivity is the reason, innovation is the key, and development is the way. The steps are simple to list, hard to carry out. The foundation of a staff development system is to capitalize on the central trait of adult learners: Adults learn best when faced with a problem. Problem-based learning is not efficient with new learners (cell 1a); first they need the facts and accumulated experience. It is, however, the most efficient method for experienced staffers. Problem-based learning challenges their constructs directly; they are not being told, lectured. They are experiencing and learning from their world and thereby enlarging their constructs.

Here is an outline of this staff development method:

1. *Challenge* experienced individuals to increase the quality of learning (or job analysis, CBT, etc.).

2. *Stimulate* with problems. Give the problems in example form.

3. *Motivate* by going over benefits to the training enterprise and what a solution means to the individual staff member (increased status, salary; decreased workload; easier life).

4. *Provide tips* on methodology. In the beginning, use the basic scientific method of defining the problem, suggesting solutions, testing solutions. Later on, move to more sophisticated designs.

5. *Support* the activity. A free innovation is worth what it costs. Provide release time, travel, reading

and research materials, consultants, data collection, brain-storming groups, or whatever is required. Also, the person may need to go back to cell 1a for retraining or advancement training.

   6. *Implement* proven solutions and give credit.

There is inevitably a limit to how much innovation a training budget can stand during a funding period. Senior management will allocate more money in next year's budget if you show the merit of innovation in improving the quality of learning.

The last goal of staff development deals with leadership and followship. To develop leadership, put the staff through the same leadership development you went through in the first part of this chapter. Add coaching, reinforcement, and perhaps a set of standards, and it will work.

Followship is a different matter. You teach everyone to be a leader; then put them in a room together. No matter how well you develop leadership, too many still think it means to dominate. Domination is not the purpose of leadership. Leadership is setting the course of the future, and it can rarely be set in our high-tech world by someone working alone. Good leadership and followship come from being *high-touch*. High-touch comes from respect and understanding others, and others are those who lead and follow.

Followship is not perceived as being as much fun or as exciting as leadership. But, too much leadership burns out individuals, and then they become disposable. Everyone needs to be a follower from time to time.

The problem in formal organizations is that we have learned to follow only persons in positions at the top of the hierarchy. Leaders are left to carry the leadership burden in their group. That's wrong. Hierarchical position does not a leader make, especially when you are surrounded with so much talent. Can you be a follower of someone below you in the hierarchical organization chart? Allow yourself to, sometime. Do you consider that as a sign of weakness? You shouldn't. Is it easier when the person is on the same level, a peer? Maybe, maybe not; try to get past that way of thinking. Are you caught up in competing for its own sake or to get ahead in the eyes of your leader? If you are, cut it out. You are cheating yourself of the opportunity to follow some talented leaders.

But, more important, HRT is too critical—too many lives are at stake, too much technology could be lost—to allow one of the classic dysfunctions of the formal organization to get in the way. The original design for organizations called for people to be promoted to higher positions because they had worked their way up, were the best. Therefore, they were the most qualified to make technically correct decisions. Does that happen today?

Training leadership can be provided. Technical leadership in training staffs must be provided at the level where it resides. The rules are simple. The leadership must be endorsed by the followship. Leadership is earned by communicating and reporting on activities completed.

Therein lies one main reason for staff meetings in training groups. Build staff meetings around the six steps of staff development: challenge, stimulate, motivate, teach methodology, support, and implement. The meetings are an excellent implementation vehicle. The process allows each member to communicate (gain a followship) and learn from having his or her reality challenged. The staff meeting is the ideal staff development greenhouse. It is a good place for you to reinforce concepts during the meeting and offer coaching before or after the meeting. All six steps can be juggled for members who are at different stages when you provide leadership. Staff meetings become vibrant, exciting activities where real business productivity, via innovation and leadership, is accomplished.

Staff development is a massive undertaking. Staff members must grow in their technical expertise and learn how to train. Development includes not only training but also movement toward better solutions to problems, which requires leadership. The fulcrum to success is recognition by all staff members that their previous styles of leadership, which used to work, will not work in training. That recognition requires a personal inventory and a resolve to monitor the environment. Training staff members at all levels need to be not only leaders in their areas of expertise but also supportive followers in other areas.

# 4
# Developing
# Procedures

Standard operating procedure, SOP, is a way of life in HRT. A painful way at times, but it is required to communicate the way you do business. Procedures control work activities and, as such, make up a communication system. Each job task taught, tested, and changed is monitored as closely as original and replacement equipment on the newest stealth aircraft. It's as important. People can often compensate for a piece of equipment—when they're trained to be knowledgeable and skillful, that is.

This chapter presents a way to develop and control written procedures, through knowing the reasons for procedures, the procedure communications cycle, procedure development and control systems, writing tips, the procedural approval cycle, and how to overcome procedure backfires.

## Reasons for Written Procedures

Written procedures give specific directions to the training staff on how to perform work and to the rest of the organization on how to obtain training services and their responsibilities in the training function. The central reason for procedures is to control work. Control is required to create and maintain consistency in the operation of training management systems such as curriculum development, instructional content delivery, testing, records input, and interaction with trainees. Control is further required to ensure that those outside training will cooperate in curriculum development and evaluations and will support training schedules.

Does this need for consistency mean that all instructors must teach alike, be robots? Absolutely not. It does mean that when the instructors step into the classroom or simulator, the instructional material has been identified and validated by the curriculum development system. It further means that the must-know information is taught. The instructor may add to content but never subtract. The instructors must integrate their experiences and make the training meaningful, based on their own creativity. Here is a specific list of reasons for written procedures. Some overlap a bit, but they interweave to form the rationale for such a communication system.

*Span of control.* When you were in the field, you were probably able to perform every job in your group. You controlled your work group by being there and making immediate, technically sound decisions. Reliability—consistency in work behavior—was caused by your presence and technical expertise.

In HRT, the breadth of technical courses taught and the software and hardware specialties required take more than one lifetime to learn. You can't look over each instructor's shoulder and know the content is exactly what should be taught. You can't look over each programmer's shoulder and tell him or her what to do next. You can't be in every learning environment to verify that the content is delivered.

So, you develop management systems so that the instructors, curriculum developers, work group supervisors, and technical experts can work together to create and validate content, deliver content, and evaluate training. Procedures tell people how to work inside the systems and give you checkpoints to make certain they have complied. HRT is serious business. It is not a college program where professors have freedom of choice over the content and methods. HRT prepares people to work in hazardous, dangerous environments. One person's judgment is not good enough.

Even if you supervise your own area of technical expertise, you will find your time siphoned away by budget concerns, curriculum meetings, staff evaluations, job analysis reviews, unit of instruction development and approval, and any other of a dozen management tasks. Procedures spread your span of control.

*Delegation of authority.* One of the oldest management practices around, delegation remains one of the most needed. Who's in charge of the simulator? Who must approve units of instruction? Who can sign for contracts? Who is held accountable? Procedures specify who makes what kind of decisions and who is accountable.

*Complexity of systems.* Curriculum development alone is a complicated system. Telling doesn't cause compliance; written direction gives the paths to follow. Procedures eliminate guesswork in determining how to interface with a complex system. Written procedures are critical not only for new staff members but also for those who infrequently work with a system.

*Organizational stability.* Written procedures ensure that the HRT function continues to perform quality work during periods of personnel turnover. One person leaving does not throw the organization into mass confusion, because procedures outlive individual incumbents.

*Documentation.* High-risk training is a low-trust environment. When incidents and accidents occur in the field, investigative bodies will be at your front door. Your word that the curriculum was well developed, properly taught, and soundly evaluated is not good enough. Your documentation must be as courtproof as possible. Well-designed procedures generate sound documentation.

*Legal and professional requirements.* HRT programs are usually associated with large complex organizations that are managed top-down by procedures. Many HRT functions are subject to investigations from external groups: regulators, licensing boards, oversight committees, elected officials, and professional associations. Most of the groups have "top-tier" procedures with which your group must show compliance, to the letter. Procedures tell how compliance is achieved and make your staff aware of top-tier procedures.

*Cause cooperation.* Supervisors of the work groups for whom you conduct training must cooperate in all phases, from curriculum development to on-the-job evaluation. A handshake won't work. A procedure formally authorized, in writing, by the supervisor's boss is the only way.

*Staff protection.* HRT staff members need procedures to keep them out of trouble. Protection is needed in many areas, but let's just take the one area of trainee testing as an example. There have been cheating scandals at all the military academies, at Three Mile Island (discovered after the accident), and at every university. Procedures on test control, administration, and confidentiality of results save pain and careers.

Written procedures are thus a method to increase control by establishing rules for reliable behavior. Although procedure development takes a tremendous amount of work, there are many benefits. The formalizing of many activities stops you from having to make the same decision over and over. It frees your time for nonstandard problems. The staff members to whom you delegate authority will increase their expertise in that area, for there is nothing like holding people accountable for a decision to make them do some homework and research. Also, if everyone is following clear and concise directions, you have a higher chance of meeting your work goals. Goals require communication.

## Procedure-Communication Cycle

What does communication mean?

The word communication originally meant to cause a common action. To accomplish a common action with procedures means that the message must be clear and understood and that it must cause work to occur in a consistent manner.

The communication cycle given in figure 9 requires a brief explanation. Although the cycle can be used to analyze oral, written, or signing (physical motioning) communication, this explanation will focus on written procedures.

Begin at twelve o'clock. The *sender* of the message is the originator of a procedure. The message goes through a *gatekeeping* function. The first gatekeeper in all communications is the sender. Ideally, the sender thinks through the capabilities of the receivers to handle the tasks and decides how much detail to put into the directions. The second set of gatekeepers is the people who review and comment on the procedure before it is published. Nothing in HRT is "one-person based." Written procedures must be reviewed by

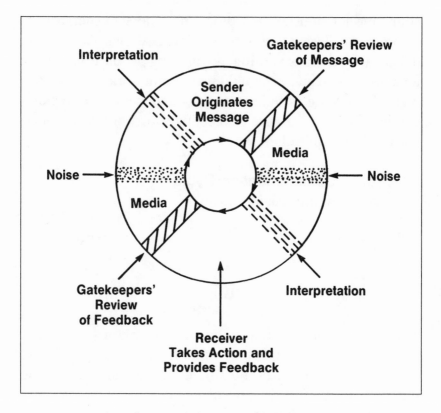

Figure 9. Communication cycle.

people who are assigned authority and responsibilities in that procedure. The reviewers either add to the procedure, leave it as is, or subtract from it. (Usually they add.)

After all the differences are worked out, the message is disseminated through *media*. The procedure is published and sent into the communications channel. Each medium has *noise*, anything that distorts communication, such as static on the car radio, lines across the TV screen, or machines operating in the workplace. Noise in procedures is caused by the limitations of the written page. You cannot show someone how to do something, only tell. You can't take a line drawing that is 11 × 17 and reduce it to 8½ × 11 without loosing detail.

The message, after gatekeeping and with its noise, is in the communications channel headed toward the *receiver*. Two points are important. One, the receiver must have *access* to the message (for example, a procedure manual). Two, the receiver must *interpret* the message. Interpreting the message is a filtering process. The receiver has to translate the terminology. In addition, receivers wear psychologically and philosophically ground eyeglasses that alter the message. The hope is that, based on the screening, the receiver takes appropriate action based on the directions. Once the actions are completed, the receiver provides *feedback* and closes the loop by sending a message back to the sender. The message goes through the same gauntlet as the original message, including interpretation.

The threats to the potency of the message are several: gatekeepers, noise, availability, and interpretation. Then there is the feedback loop with the same threats. Let's look at a system that addresses these issues.

## Procedure Development and Control System

There are two broad classifications of needed procedures: (1) internal procedures, where all responsibilities are accomplished inside the training division (only HRT staff members need access) and (2) external-internal procedures, where personnel outside training have responsibility to cooperate with the HRT staff (both groups need access). Both types of procedures can be developed in the same manner.

In training, you work with people, programs, data, and things:

| People: | Programs: |
|---|---|
| Staff | Training Programs |
| Trainees | Development Programs |
| Key Organization People | Certification Programs |

| Data: | Things: |
|---|---|
| People | Facilities |
| Programs | Equipment Maintenance |
| Things | Enhancements |

You manage the development, operation, evaluation, and improvement of the four areas. There is no single neat matrix that defines the procedural needs of the areas. Thus, to come up with an absolute list of procedure needs for HRT is improbable. Procedures could be written for the interaction of any combination of those areas and tasks. Just to give an indication, figures 10 and 11 present two sample tables of contents. Note how the distribution of procedures varies to suit the differing needs of user groups.

In figure 10, section 1 would give explicit details needed by the staff on curriculum subsystems. Section 2 would show the steps required to become fully qualified in specific jobs. Section 3 would tell how to interface with the procedure system. Section 4 would detail how to work with records. Section 5 would describe how to conduct an evaluation and be evaluated. Section 6 would specify administrative requirements.

In figure 11, section 1 would identify how the curriculum systems work and identify all responsible parties inside and outside the training division. Section 2 would identify the details of entrance, curriculum, and completion of all training programs. Section 3 would give roles for evaluation of the programs. Section 4 would tell how to obtain services.

These are mere examples. You may only have five procedures, or you may have to work with two hundred. Five

SECTION 1    CURRICULUM DEVELOPMENT
             1.1   Job Analysis System
             1.2   Unit of Instruction Format
             1.3   Scenario Format
             1.4   Instructional Material Change Process
             1.5   Instructional Material Storage and Copying
                   Process

SECTION 2    STAFF DEVELOPMENT
             2.1   Instructor Certification Program
             2.2   Training Specialist Certification Program
             2.3   Supervisor Certification Program

SECTION 3    PROCEDURE PROGRAM
             3.1   Procedure Development
             3.2   Procedure Distribution and Control
             3.3   Procedure Change System

SECTION 4    TRAINING RECORDS PROGRAM
             4.1   Records Configurations Control
             4.2   Records Access Control
             4.3   Records Report Schedule

SECTION 5    EVALUATION
             5.1   Curriculum Evaluation
             5.2   Staff Evaluation
             5.3   Procedure Evaluation
             5.4   Training Records Evaluation

SECTION 6    STAFF ADMINISTRATION
             6.1   Sickness
             6.2   Support for Professional Development
             6.3   Grievance System

Figure 10. Example of HRT internal procedures.

probably means the organization doesn't take you seriously. Two hundred probably means the organization is scared. You need the number and type of procedures that you need. No more, no less.

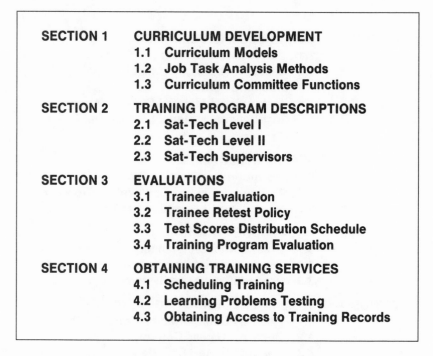

| | |
|---|---|
| **SECTION 1** | **CURRICULUM DEVELOPMENT** |
| | **1.1  Curriculum Models** |
| | **1.2  Job Task Analysis Methods** |
| | **1.3  Curriculum Committee Functions** |
| **SECTION 2** | **TRAINING PROGRAM DESCRIPTIONS** |
| | **2.1  Sat-Tech Level I** |
| | **2.2  Sat-Tech Level II** |
| | **2.3  Sat-Tech Supervisors** |
| **SECTION 3** | **EVALUATIONS** |
| | **3.1  Trainee Evaluation** |
| | **3.2  Trainee Retest Policy** |
| | **3.3  Test Scores Distribution Schedule** |
| | **3.4  Training Program Evaluation** |
| **SECTION 4** | **OBTAINING TRAINING SERVICES** |
| | **4.1  Scheduling Training** |
| | **4.2  Learning Problems Testing** |
| | **4.3  Obtaining Access to Training Records** |

Figure 11. Example of HRT external-internal procedures.

## Writing and Readability

The procedure development and distribution system can be best expressed in a sample procedure on how to develop and distribute procedures. The Appendix gives a procedure on developing procedures. What you include in a procedure depends, of course, on what you want to accomplish with the procedure. Let's look at some tips on writing procedures.

There are two schools of thought about who should write a procedure. One advocates that it should be written by the most technically experienced individual. The other believes in selecting someone more junior, which not only overcomes the problem of an experienced person leaving out a step performed unconsciously but also provides good training and learning for the junior person. There's probably a third school that says a committee should generate the procedure.

Although the situation will differ, take a lesson from Napoleon. He would create a battle order, call in a private, and give the order. If the private understood it, he would send it to his generals. Have your best person write the procedure. Then see if the most junior person can follow the instructions. The approval chain will provide a committee-type review. It results in faster product turnaround and builds an understanding of procedure development with the junior person. The junior will learn during the tryout, and the experience is good preparation for future procedure development, which in turn will relieve the senior person from doing all the procedure development.

Whoever is writing the procedure needs some guidance on the nature of procedure writing. Here are some principles.

1. *Procedures stand alone.* From the title, which must clearly identify the topic, to the last phrase, other explanations are not needed.

2. *Procedures are instructions.* The verbiage is not for giving descriptions or suggestions. Cold, factual, to-the-point instructions are required. For example:

| Incorrect | Correct |
|---|---|
| 1. You must place the simulator in the freeze mode before going to the slow-ahead mode or the location in the scenario will be lost and you will have to rerun up to the point where you were, unless you need to review the scenario with. . . | 1. Depress the freeze mode key. 2. Depress slow-ahead mode key. |

3. *Instructions must be short.* They must be devoid of extra words. For example:

| Incorrect | Correct |
|---|---|
| 1. If the indicator is set on 1, the simulator is ready for full-scope simulation. | 1. Set indicator on 1 for full-scope simulation. |
| 2. If the indicator is set on 2, the simulator annunciators are turned off. | 2. Set indicator on 2 to turn off annunciators. |

4. *Few illustrations are self-explanatory.* They are equal partners with words. A few extra words will often do the trick. For example:

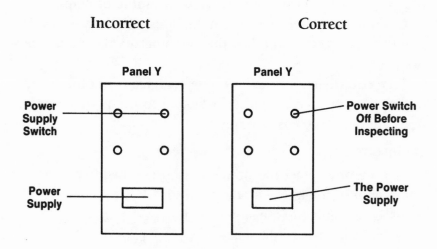

5. *Use a standard language for options.* It must be taught to all writers and users. A hierarchy established by federal codes and used by professional organizations is—

Shall = mandatory
Should = recommended
May = choice

| Incorrect | Correct |
|---|---|
| 1. You should always turn the simulator off during a power outage. | 1. The operator shall turn the simulator off during a power outage. |
| 2. It's strongly suggested that you wait 30 minutes before restarting the simulator after power is restored. | 2. The operator should wait 30 minutes before restarting the simulator after power is recovered. |
| 3. At this point you might decide to record the outage, including length of time, who was in training, etc. | 3. The operator may log the outage. |

6. *Write procedures for users.* Procedures are written for the people who have to carry out the instructions. Too often writers create documents for their peers. A software engineer writing a startup procedure for the simulator must be reminded that instructors are the users.

7. *There is a trade-off between conciseness and reading levels.* Short sentences usually contribute to a lower reading level. Long sentences filled with technical jargon raise the reading level. When in doubt, go for the lower reading level by using one-concept sentences.

Once a procedure is written, the next step is to gain procedure approval.

## Procedure Approval Cycle

A procedure system requires top-down approval for success, like any other organizational system. Beyond the top-down endorsement, the system is only as good as the endorsement of those assigned responsibilities in that section of the procedure. As shown in figure 12, the cycle is simple.

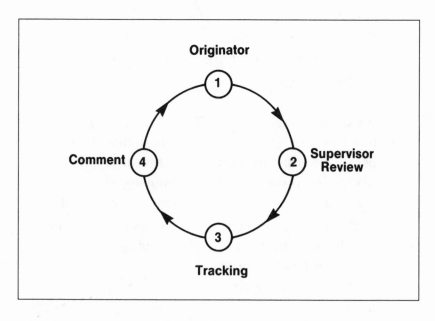

Figure 12. Procedure approval cycle.

It has four basic steps:

1. Originator submits draft to supervisor.

2. Supervisor reviews and, generally after some revision, submits it into the tracking system.

3. Tracking system logs it in, assigns a due date, and forwards it to reviewers.

4. Reviewers comment and send to originator.

After the originator of a procedure receives reviewers' comments, the cycle begins again. This time, the originator attempts to resolve comments while maintaining the integrity of the procedure.

If the procedure cycles more than twice, training management must intervene, using the four approaches of authority, power, persuasion, and training (chapter 1). Sometimes some of the reviewers refuse to sign off on a procedure. Usually their concern is the time employees must devote to comply with the procedure. (Technical issues, on the other hand, are generally resolved early on.) Thrashing someone to get a procedure signed is poor business. Additional work may indeed require additional resources. If you propose to lay more workload on a work group, you must also raise the problem of resources to senior management.

Once the procedure cover sheet is signed off by all parties with responsibilities, the original is placed into a depository (fireproof cabinets). Copies are made and stamped *Controlled* in red ink as a precaution. Suppose someone pulls a procedure from a manual and makes a personal desk copy. The red ink shows up black, and it always reminds that person and anyone else who sees it that they had better check the nearest manual to see if it is the current procedure. Although manual holders are always cautioned not to make copies, it frequently happens in the distribution chain.

## How Procedures Can Backfire

We implement control systems of various types in an organization to gain reliability and cause accountability. We wouldn't do it unless we anticipated success. With written procedures, the consequences we anticipate usually occur. But, for every action there is a reaction. There are unanticipated consequences, things we didn't plan to occur. Specific backfires are, of course, often caused by specific procedures (which you try to forecast and fix, or fix after you discover).

Nevertheless, there are some broad dysfunctions to most control systems:

- Procedures provide cues to minimum acceptable behavior: "I did just what the procedure said."

- Delegation of authority to subgroups can lead each group to develop its own "compartment" and forget they're part of a larger team: "Hey, that's not our problem."

- Client dissatisfaction can result when procedures are used as an excuse for inaction: "I can't do anything, my hands are tied."

- Procedures can be manipulated by incumbents to give them a secure, do-nothing job or an "I've got to approve everything" attitude (maybe more a fault of management style than procedures).

- Decreased innovation may occur because everything is spelled out and seems to work: "I can't do that because. . . ." Or, "I never even noticed that. . . ."

- Procedures can become the easy solution for weak managers. Every time someone does something wrong, instead of applying supervisory skills, a new procedure is written or one is revised. This approach increases the sheer volume of procedures to the point of confusion. It also results in roadblocks being placed in the way of getting day-to-day business accomplished.

In addition to these typical backfires are the uses that auditing groups, internal and external, have for procedures. You write and approve the procedure. You are audited on your compliance with your procedures. Deviations result in audit findings, which at a minimum require a written response and, with regulatory agencies, can result in substantial fines.

The way to win with auditors and inspectors is to have good procedures that you indeed follow. How to beat unanticipated consequences is less clear. There are some actions you can take:

- Teach staff members that procedures are not set in stone. Procedures capture the best way to do an activity. When a better way is found, the procedure needs to be revised. Never follow a procedure when it's wrong. Stop and get it changed.

- Put mandatory revision time frames on all procedures, such as every six months on a technical procedure and every year on an administrative procedure.

- Monitor the environment intensely for dysfunctions and misuse.

- Keep reminding the staff that they are responsible for initiating changes: "Don't become slaves to a piece of paper. . . ."

- Reinforce innovation and procedures as the way to implement change.

You can never beat all the possible dysfunctions of procedures. But you can minimize the cost of backfires and make good procedures a full-time management concern.

Procedures are necessary to control the diversity of an HRT function, promote cooperation from groups served, and implement higher-level mandates. Rigid control brings with it, however, the costs of reducing innovations and building fences between groups. Management attention is required to mitigate those costs.

Procedures are concise instructions, not prose. Practice is required to generate a quality procedure. It is more than worthwhile; having the correct procedures in place in the hands of the right people may save lives.

# 5
# Developing Records

Records are documentation of what an HRT function has done. In HRT, not knowing what you have done is a clear statement that you don't know what you're doing. Your focus on records is of equal importance to curriculum, staff, and procedure development. Without a superior records system, you cannot provide documentation when, where, and in the configuration needed.

This chapter presents a way to develop a records system. You must understand the reasons for and uses of documentation, how to identify what needs to be documented, the structure and function of a documentation system, budget links, and automation of the system.

## Reasons for Documentation

The concept of documentation is particularly close to the heart of a trainer. The original root of the word was *docere*, to teach. The word evolved to *documenium*, to teach a lesson of proof. The real meaning of the word is more than a stack of papers:

| DOCUMENT | | ATION |
|:---:|:---:|:---:|
| ↓ | | ↓ |
| CONCRETE | ON | CONDITION |
| LESSON | | OF BEING |

Documentation is teaching by proving how things are. There are reasons you must perform in such a specified manner.

Records are concerned with valid and specific factual data that can be immediately accessed for use in three areas:

1. *Day-to-day business.* You need to know who was trained on what, when they were trained, and how well the learning was accomplished. You will need more than a transcript service. *When* may be five years ago. *What* doesn't mean the unit of instruction used today, but the exact revision used five years ago. *How well* the learning was accomplished doesn't mean just a score on a printout but the exact test paper or evaluation sheets. Documentation proves qualifications for job assignments, certifications, promotions, and entry to advancement training.

2. *Training center business.* You need to be able to demonstrate accomplishments, failures, and the cost of each. Business changes are driven by those three items. Building the annual budget and justifying it requires knowing how many were trained and their performance on evaluations as well as on the job. Curriculum modifications are often driven by failures. Documentation must answer who failed, where they failed, and perhaps even why.

3. *Investigation business.* Investigations are a part of the routine and panic in HRT. All investigations are serious. Some carry more gravity than others. An annual internal audit will seek documentation that procedures are up to date and followed. An external audit or panic internal audits are typically witch-hunts conducted for one of three reasons: (1) to protect the public, (2) to protect the workers, or (3) to place blame because of an accident. These audits can come from regulatory agencies, congressional committees, or interveners represented by lawyers and supported by the court.

Investigations, when operated by professional auditors, can only help an HRT function. A quality I.G. inspection, a well-designed internal audit, or a sincere effort to protect the public are useful audits that help you do your work better. A witch-hunt by people with vested interests and absurd guidelines can be devastating to a good program. In any case, your protection is documentation—proof, if you will, legal evidence—that will stand up to the rules of evidence in a court of law. A simple stack of papers will not accomplish that level of confidence. You must have proper documentation.

Good documentation is a friend when you really need a friend. Poor documentation is always an enemy. When a worker has a loss-of-common-sense accident and cops out by saying, "I wasn't trained on that," you will find out the real failure. Quality, courtproof records are no accident. The place to begin structuring the records system is with the curriculum development models in chapter 2. But, you will have to do more, because monies invested in training records must benefit the entire system.

## Areas of Documentation

You don't want to spend your entire career on documentation. Nor do you want to let other training leaders drift off and make it a career. As much as it appeals to some personality types, documentation is merely a part of the lives of all HRT staff members. The staff responsible for records are the skilled professionals trained in records management; everyone else supports them. Make sure your staff understands this principle. They may need reminding if a supervisor, for example, falls into the self-appointed role of being the enforcer of quality records. It is everyone's task, a part of the job. To allow it to fall to a "mother" will cause the staff to feel it is no longer part of their work: "Wait until so-and-so screams; then we'll send it in." This state of mind is not needed in the training staff. Documentation is a part of everyone's job.

To develop the basic record system requires integration of Models 1 and 2 (chapter 2) with monies expended. Each model has outcomes in each block that become inputs to the records system. There are five tiers of documentation from the curriculum models. Figure 13 reflects these areas.

A walk-down of figure 13 is more meaningful with a facility, furniture, software, and hardware in mind. Assume you have a records room (see figure 14). Against one wall is a series of six five-drawer, fireproof file cabinets (watch out for the old ones that were insulated with asbestos). Against another wall are CRTs and keyboards that access the mainframe or powerful PCs, including printers. The third wall has micro-fiche and microfilm storage with readers that can make hard copies. You may have more or less than this imagined records room. What counts is the concept of storage and retrieval.

Data are stored in three ways: hard copy (in file cabinets), microfiche and microfilm (transferred from hard copy), and on a computer data base. The only reason to store data is to retrieve the data. Data that never need to be retrieved never need to be stored.

Let's suppose you have five curriculums, one for each drawer in a five-drawer file cabinet. A front view of the file cabinet wall is shown in figure 15. Now let's walk down figure 13 and place the documentation in the records room (figure 14), in the configuration shown in figure 15 (for our example of a sat-tech curriculum). Let's start with the first file cabinet in our imaginary records room, Curriculum Foundation (13.1).

13.1.1 *Needs of Trainees.* All data that describe the typical trainee are grouped. The data will be added to and recalculated as new trainees enter. The reason for the file (data base) is

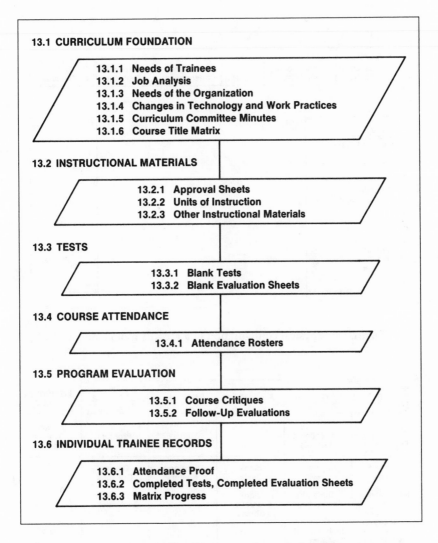

**13.1 CURRICULUM FOUNDATION**

13.1.1 Needs of Trainees
13.1.2 Job Analysis
13.1.3 Needs of the Organization
13.1.4 Changes in Technology and Work Practices
13.1.5 Curriculum Committee Minutes
13.1.6 Course Title Matrix

**13.2 INSTRUCTIONAL MATERIALS**

13.2.1 Approval Sheets
13.2.2 Units of Instruction
13.2.3 Other Instructional Materials

**13.3 TESTS**

13.3.1 Blank Tests
13.3.2 Blank Evaluation Sheets

**13.4 COURSE ATTENDANCE**

13.4.1 Attendance Rosters

**13.5 PROGRAM EVALUATION**

13.5.1 Course Critiques
13.5.2 Follow-Up Evaluations

**13.6 INDIVIDUAL TRAINEE RECORDS**

13.6.1 Attendance Proof
13.6.2 Completed Tests, Completed Evaluation Sheets
13.6.3 Matrix Progress

Figure 13. Curriculum tiers for records input.

to judge significant differences in an entering class from previous classes. The data include reading levels, intelligence scores, physical conditions, etc. (see chapter 2).

13.1.2 *Job Analysis.* For hands-on purposes a current print-out should be maintained in the file. Instructors need a fresh

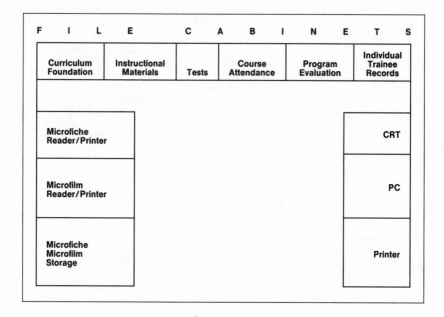

| F I L E | C A B I N E T S | | | | |
|---|---|---|---|---|---|
| Curriculum Foundation | Instructional Materials | Tests | Course Attendance | Program Evaluation | Individual Trainee Records |

Figure 14. Physical configuration of a records room (top view).

| P R O G R A M | F I L E S | | | | INDIVIDUAL FILES |
|---|---|---|---|---|---|
| Curriculum Foundation | Instructional Materials | Tests | Course Attendance | Program Evaluation | Individual Trainee Records |
| Trainee's Needs — Job Analysis — Organization's Needs — Technology and Work Practice Changes — Curriculum Committee Minutes — Course Title Matrix | Approval Sheets — Units of Instruction — Other Instructional Material | Blank Tests — Blank Evaluation Sheets | Attendance Rosters | Course Critiques — Follow-Up Evaluations | A-Z |

Figure 15. File cabinet contents for HRT records.

working copy. In making changes to instructional materials and tracking job task changes to objectives, instructors will continually use the file. Auditors, in tracking what is taught and why, will also use the file.

13.1.3 *Needs of the Organization.* This base document is also a tracking file. It describes the job and pending changes.

13.1.4 *Changes to Technology and Work Practices.* This file is a major documentation point. It is a busy file, because its purpose is tracking changes.

13.1.5 *Curriculum Committee Minutes.* Minutes are filed for proof of consensus and updated to show the attention of the committee to program evaluations and other activities such as accidents.

13.1.6 *Course Titles.* Course objectives from the curriculum committee are organized into a matrix. The matrix shows the interrelationship of courses to job titles. Figure 16 is an example. These matrices are of utmost importance in the interrelationship of people to programs and attainment of full certification. Inside a records program, the progress of trainees through a matrix can predict the next year's training budget needs.

Now let's look at the second file cabinet in figure 15, Instructional Materials (13.2), which encompasses three types of materials.

13.2.1 *Approval Sheets.* Each unit of instruction must be approved by the technical and work group supervisors and other parties, including the instructor, supervisor of instruction, and manager of training. Evidence is dated signatures on the cover sheets.

13.2.2 *Units of Instruction.* These instructional materials are in a continual state of revision. An instructor can't borrow one from another instructor. It won't be current. Nor can an instructor pull out last year's presentation and know it is the

| Sat-Techs | Basic Electronics and Electricity | Instruments and Controls | Measuring Devices | Millimeter Wave Radar | Supervisory Skills |
|---|---|---|---|---|---|
| Level I | R | R | R | * | * |
| Level II | S | R | R | R | S |
| Supervisory Level | S | R | R | R | R |

R = Required     S = Suggested     * = Not Needed

Figure 16. Sat-tech curriculum matrix.

latest revision. This file contains the most current units of instruction. Only from this file are copies made for each class.

13.2.3 *Other Instructional Materials.* This category is a quagmire that is difficult to control. One course is accompanied by a videotape. Another is supported by a textbook. Don't try to maintain a copy of those instructional materials here (use your library). What is needed in this file is a current reference list and the location of the referenced items.

Now let's turn to the third file cabinet, Tests (13.3), which contains both blank tests and blank evaluation sheets.

13.3.1 *Blank Tests.* Based on the objectives of each unit of instruction, tests are maintained, as is everything else, under strict controls. Test control is even more strict. There is no one-person entry. Dual entry is minimum. All entries require a sign-in log. All entries must be observed by a supervisor.

No matter how hard you try, someone will attempt to breach this system. Not pretty, not right, but it happens. Breaches of these records have occurred at all military academies, at every major university, and on government tests. You must be defensive and offensive. Any control system you can implement, someone will figure out how to break. The best way to treat the test file is as if it contains life-threatening information or your income tax records.

13.3.2 *Blank Evaluation Sheets.* These sheets are of less concern. They are filled in by instructors during simulation, lab, shop, or field activities. The effort here is to ensure that the forms are the most current.

The fourth file cabinet, Course Attendance (13.4), contains the attendance rosters (13.4.1), which are proof of attendance and the starting point for individual trainee records. Figure 17 is an example of a simple, in-the-classroom roster. The social security number is critical for tracking in an automated (computerized) system.

The fifth file cabinet in our records room contains materials on Program Evaluation (13.5).

13.5.1 *End-of-Course Critiques.* These critiques have a short-life usefulness, and you may establish a six-month file life for them. (Part 3 of this book covers evaluation in depth.)

13.5.2 *Follow-Up Evaluations.* These evaluations are for feedback that goes to the curriculum committee. The evaluations can drive curriculum change or provide documentation for remaining constant. They are long-term data base documents so that each new evaluation can be compared to previous evaluations.

Page _____ of _____

HRT TRAINING ROSTER (Black Ink Only)

| Course Title and Unit of Instruction Number | Beginning Date | | Ending Date | | | | | | | |
|---|---|---|---|---|---|---|---|---|---|---|
| | | | | | | | | | | |

| Printed Name | Signature | Soc. Sec. No. | S | M | T | W | T | F | S | Test Score |
|---|---|---|---|---|---|---|---|---|---|---|
| | | | | | | | | | | |
| | | | | | | | | | | |
| | | | | | | | | | | |
| | | | | | | | | | | |
| | | | | | | | | | | |
| | | | | | | | | | | |
| | | | | | | | | | | |
| | | | | | | | | | | |
| | | | | | | | | | | |
| | | | | | | | | | | |
| | | | | | | | | | | |
| | | | | | | | | | | |
| | | | | | | | | | | |

Instructor's Signature                                    Date

Figure 17.  HRT training roster.

Those five areas—the contents of the first five file cabinets—complete the program side of your documentation, providing proof of what is in the curriculum and why, to whom it was taught, and when. The next section, Individual Training Records (13.6), in the sixth file cabinet, proves how well each trainee did and where each training course fits into the individual's program.

13.6.1 *Proof of Attendance.* A copy of the attendance roster may be placed inside each individual file. But that tends to become a bit bulky in an active program. A simple solution is to record the course on an individual form and have the input clerk initial and date the entry. The original black-ink signature on the attendance roster resides in the next file and can easily be cross-indexed.

13.6.2 *Completed Tests and Evaluations.* These pieces of information are the most confidential in the records system. Not only is a certain morality involved in protecting the rights of the individual, but such confidentiality is required by state and federal privacy laws and several court rulings. You must have a control procedure (chapter 4) covering access to these records. Besides the individual, others who would have access include the person's supervisor, the input clerk, selected members of the training staff, and auditors. You should not allow these files to leave the records room. Copying the contents should never be allowed, even by the individual; besides protecting the individual's right to privacy, you must not allow the security of a current test to be breached.

13.6.3 *Matrix Progress.* For each trainee, you must maintain a copy of the training matrix where courses completed are checked off. Not only is this document valuable for the individual, but training matrices, collectively, can be used for forecasting and scheduling courses.

In its entirety, figure 13 presents one subsystem of a total documentation system. Before discussing how to manage, automate, and reduce the bulk of paper, let's look at the budget subsystem.

### Budget Links

A budget, by any definition, is the way you carry out a plan. You need to develop a budget-linking system that associates a cost with each training center function. By knowing your costs in that manner, you more professionally build and justify next year's budget. The problem is that your budget, which is set up using overall organizational budget terms, will not be in the same configuration as your training functions. For example, salaries are usually classified as one line item. You will have to establish a system that will accurately assign time, and thus dollars, to instructional time, curriculum development time, course development time, and so forth. The task is, fortunately for you, not that difficult.

A typical organization budget has three major items:

- *Capital items*: Expenditures for new equipment, facility expansion, or renovation.

- *Operations costs*: Day-to-day costs of running the training function, such as leases on computers, copiers, and perhaps phone systems; janitorial and maintenance costs; replacement tools; equipment repair; consultant costs; books and tapes.

- *Salaries*: Remuneration costs that may be broken down by some division of management and bargaining unit personnel or perhaps by grade or rank.

Tracking training costs requires you to develop a more exact listing of line items and the staff to report how they spend their time. *Capital items* can be broken out by programs; for example, expansion of the physical space for the sat-tech program is a one-time cost prorated over the life expectancy of the improvement. *Operations costs* fall into two categories: (1) those identifiable for a specific program (e.g., tools for the sat-tech program) or (2) those classified as overhead and spread proportionally over all programs (e.g., copying machine costs). *Salary expenses*, for your purposes, must be tracked by having each individual record the time invested in each daily activity.

You will need a classification scheme for tracking how staff members spend their time. For example—

Instructional Staff
1.0 Curriculum Development
2.0 Instructional Materials Development
3.0 Instruction
4.0 Trainee Testing and Evaluation
5.0 Program Evaluation
6.0 Administration

Additional details may be added, such as—

3.0 Instruction
    3.1 Classroom
    3.2 Simulator
    3.3 OJT Supervision
    3.4 CBT Supervision

The more details involved, the more cumbersome the tracking becomes. You are not conducting a time-and-motion study. You are striving to develop a manageable system of associating a cost to a process, to develop a product for budget building and justification. Support personnel salaries may be calculated and prorated across the programs.

You can fairly easily teach the staff how to track their time. The problem comes in managing the vast amounts of data. Automation and paper reduction usually require software assistance.

## Automation and Paper Reduction

Tracking all this data, you could generate an enormous bulk of paper that may need to be kept for years. What you need is records management. For example, outdated revisions of units of instruction are not useful to instructors but are to auditors and lawyers. Files of past employees may be needed in some future legal issue but have no day-to-day function. There is a solution. It is, however, site specific and will vary depending on your needs and obligations. Here are some points to consider.

*Transfer.* Deciding what to microfiche or film, and when, can only be answered locally. In some cases, everything is filmed and sent to another storage site. In case of accident, the film copies will be usable. In other systems, anything replaced with a newer revision is filmed and stored on site.

*Duality.* You must have two ways to get basically the same information. For example, the paper files on each trainee are placed on a mainframe with limited access allowed. Via social security numbers, a job planner can access the file to determine if an employee is trained to work on a specific job. No test scores are shown, only a final grade of complete or incomplete. Exact test scores reside in the paper file. This type of a system, using training matrices, can allow the computer to forecast training schedules.

*Integration.* You must match the storage type (paper, film, computer) to the files it best handles. All job analyses are on the computer and printed out as needed. Earlier revisions are archived. All blank tests and evaluations are maintained in a paper file.

*Reporting capabilities.* This area is the most difficult to predict for a system. Asking yourself what kinds of reports are needed will identify the obvious. Supervisors need monthly reports on employees whose certifications or licenses are going to expire within the next ninety days. You need to accumulate day-to-day costs for budget building. Instructors need reports on revision dates of units. Trainees need basic reports of where they are and how far they need to go. Senior managers may require overall status reports on the state of training of the work force. You may decide to bring in a committee and do some trial report development.

Software development is expensive. You can help keep costs down by anticipating the answers to some of the questions the programmers will probably ask as they plan your system:

- What are the environmental factors that may affect the system?
- What are the data to be processed?
- How do the data enter the system?
- How are the data recorded?
- For what are the data used?
- Who gets the data, for what purpose, and in what volume?
- What is the normal data volume?
- What are the normal and peak load periods?
- What procedures must be used during system failure?

The software professionals will want the system description as specific as possible. You will want as much flexibility as possible. Your committee must be as farsighted as possible, because redefining the purpose once programming has started is costly and will push back the completion date. Calls or visits to other training sites—even if the training is of some other type—can pay major dividends.

Records are of equal importance to all other functions. They prove what you have done and can assist in forecasting future demands, and they are used in day-to-day operations and for audit purposes. Ideas can be gained from other sites, although you will almost certainly not be able to borrow a system lock, stock, and barrel. And, remember, to develop or retrofit an automated system, you will probably need outside assistance.

Developing curriculum, staff, procedures, and records is an ongoing job; something is always being developed. Meanwhile, you have to be implementing and utilizing the existing systems—a balancing act indeed. In Part 2, Utilizing, chapters 6 through 9 demonstrate ways to achieve balance through quality management.

# Part 2: Utilizing

The efficiency and effectiveness of training rests in how well the developed plans are *utilized*. The day-to-day life in a training center need not be a mass of scheduling changes, aborted programs, and disgruntled trainees. The function of a training center is to train, which means changing people, an awesome responsibility. Training is sometimes resisted by trainees and, amazingly, their supervisors. The processes go easier when day-to-day activities operate smoothly.

There are many ways to enhance traditional implementation and utilization methods and gain extra productivity from your training systems. Chapter 6, Utilizing Curriculum, tells how to organize, package, schedule, and deliver a curriculum. These steps may sound easy, but if you have tried to put a schedule together and get trainees there, you know it's not simple. The chapter also critiques the strengths and weaknesses of each delivery method. Chapter 7, Utilizing Staff, digs deeper into the operation of a training center by frankly addressing where the training organization should be located in the organization, and it presents ways to estimate the size of staff needed based on estimates of workload, some innovative ways to organize the staff to fit the technology of training, and ways to increase production through individual work plans. Chapter 8, Utilizing Procedures, is another nuts-and-bolts chapter. It concentrates on how to introduce new staff members to the practice of working with procedures, how to make certain everyone gets the word on procedure changes, how to enforce the use of procedures, and when and how to make exceptions to changes. Chapter 9, Utilizing Records, is a major step forward because it shows how to use records to build productivity by generating performance indicators. The thrust of the chapter is on the design, packaging, and distribution of the indicators that show how well training is meeting all its goals. Performance indicators are excellent devices for communicating accomplishments and needs and for your own tracking of how well the training function is performing.

# 6
# Utilizing Curriculum

A curriculum is a product, in one sense. Like any product, it does no good on the shelf. Once taken off the shelf it can be misused. A quality curriculum is an expensive product. Its use must be well planned and controlled to receive a worthwhile return on the investment.

This chapter presents ways to utilize the curriculum. You must learn to organize, package, schedule, and deliver the curriculum in a safe fashion.

## Organization

Organizing the curriculum begins in the curriculum development process (chapter 2) when individual courses are identified. Little organization is left to be accomplished if you are fortunate enough to be in the following situation:

> All trainees arrive at the same time for the same lock-step initial curriculum. After completing it, they cycle in and out of retraining and continuous training on a prescribed basis. In advancement training, they essentially become your personnel for the length of the curriculum.

However, you will need further organization and articulation of the curriculum if you are in the following situation:

Employees are hired whenever openings occur. They are assigned the job position of helper. They have three years in which to become certified (complete initial training). The total length of the curriculum is twelve weeks and is made up of seventeen courses. The courses vary in length from four hours to thirty-two hours. Work requirements do not allow all helpers (who are at various stages of completing the program) to be released for training at the same time.

You are probably in the latter situation, with timing and the demands of trainees' work highly variable. Training supervisors facing this situation commonly go immediately into a scheduling frenzy—too big a jump. By organizing the curriculum first, you can simplify the scheduling process and allow the training function to better support the personnel.

When the curriculum was originally developed, it was viewed as a straight-line progression track, and rightly so. Organizing the curriculum means taking a thoughtful look to see if some "paralleling" can be done. Let's suppose twelve weeks of training fall into three neat segments:

- Basic courses meant to get everyone up to the same level on math, science, physics, and theory

- Intermediate courses on nomenclature, function, and replacing parts

- High-tech courses on troubleshooting and diagnostics

Inside each one of those blocks are levels of complexity, such as low, medium, and high. Using figure 18 as a classification

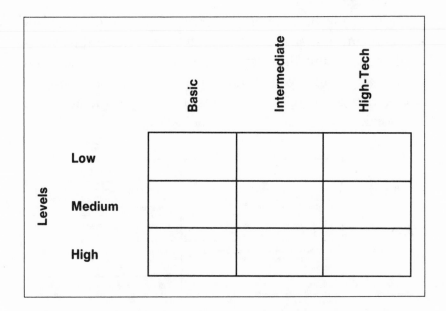

Figure 18. Matrix for paralleling courses.

tool, you can plug the seventeen courses into the appropriate cells.

Now you have established prerequisites and reduced the number of courses to be scheduled from seventeen to nine as far as trainee entry and control are concerned. Which course in a block they take first doesn't matter, but the blocks still build on each other. Paralleling the courses will add flexibility to your program. Sometimes minor course modifications might be required. The use of figure 18 is also a step forward in packaging your curriculum.

## Packaging

Packaging the curriculum by teaching style (lecture, simulation, etc.) began in the course development phase of curriculum development. Judgments were made on which package was within the capabilities of the training staff and facilities while best fitting the content. You should always question the initial judgments. After the curriculum is implemented, maintain a day-to-day vigilance of courses with an eye to whether you should change course packaging as needs change. Figure 19 presents a review of the strengths and weaknesses of each type of packaging.

| | Advantages | Disadvantages |
|---|---|---|
| Lecture | Enables the economical transmission of vast amounts of content to large groups. | Has poor interaction rate. (Trainees can get by without having their constructs challenged.) |
| Lecture and Discussion | Allows and forces trainees to interact. Challenges constructs. | Works best with small groups. Slow. Easy to get off track. |
| Laboratory or Shop | Allows hands-on demonstration and requires trainee to show competence. | Has low instructor-to-trainee ratio. Expensive. |
| OJT or Internship | Allows trainee to learn in actual work environment through a hands-on method. | Difficult to control and ensure that the trainee is learning the right methods (content). |
| Self-Study | Does not interfere with work. | Depends on trainees' self-discipline. |
| CBT | Forces interaction of trainee with content. Easy to schedule. Tracks learner progress through program. Shortens course time. | Expensive to develop. Must be proctored. |
| Part-Task Simulation | Puts learner in "no-risk" environment where interaction occurs with mock parts or situations that can or will occur on the job. Excellent for teaching subsystem interaction. | Only a portion of the environment is simulated. Costly. |
| Full-Scope Simulation | Puts learner in complete environment without risk to trainee or equipment or instructor. Makes the learner prove application of knowledge in real-time situations. | Expensive in initial cost and requires continual upgrading. |
| Field Simulation | Puts trainee in actual environment for instructors to judge trainee's application of knowledge. | Usually results in scheduling problems. Climate may interfere with learning. Some equipment and techniques may not be used for safety and expense reasons. |

Figure 19. Advantages and disadvantages of different types of course packaging.

Just as a curriculum is modified to keep up with changes, the packaging should always be reviewed to see if it is in step. Using a progression of the packages in each course can maximize learning. For example—

1. Use lecture to cover the basics and get everyone to the same theoretical level.

2. Use lab or shop to provide hands-on experiences.

3. Use lecture and discussion to go over lessons learned and how to handle the unusual.

4. Use simulation to demonstrate application of knowledge and skills in decision-making situations.

That type of a progression builds on how adults learn (hearing, hands-on, discussion, action). It also matches adults' learning curve of simple to complex.

One modification to the packaging is to add a simulation experience or demonstration before the lecture. The purpose is to immediately penetrate the trainees' construct. Gaining their attention in this manner can be a bit risky if the trainees are endangered or embarrassed (it can alienate them as learners). Basic judgment and respect for trainees can make it a worthwhile approach.

Cost-effectiveness is another reason for always being alert to the way a curriculum is packaged and repackaged. Consider a lecture in the initial curriculum that presents material that is not only difficult but often quickly forgotten. Leaving the lecture in place, the material is converted into a CBT package. The package then provides a second learning situation for the trainees in the initial curriculum and becomes part of the retraining program. It saves a lecture in the retraining curriculum and provides backup in the initial curriculum.

Similarly, a continuous review of how content is packaged can pay dividends. What began as a one-hour lecture can become a ten-minute lab demonstration when learning rates are proven to remain the same. Packaging, like curriculum, is never completed. Neither is scheduling.

## Scheduling

If there is a science to scheduling, it has yet to be discovered. We can talk, however, about two levels of scheduling. One level might be called critical time frames of learning. The other level confirms dates, times, places.

The idea of critical time frames may refute the Arabic saying, "You can't lead an old camel down a new trail" and the Western world saying, "You can't teach an old dog new tricks." Both sayings are often wrong when applied to (1) stressful situations and (2) adult learners. Timing and motivational issues are crucial. When thirsty, the old camel will learn a' new trail to an oasis.

Adults are problem-based learners. They learn best just before they face a major task. They become motivated. Teaching a group of thirty people to do a critical task six months before the task is to be done is not good scheduling. Nor is bringing in totally new, naive trainees and locking them away in training for six or twelve weeks before they see the real size and scope of the demands of the job. Trainees need "pegs" on which to hang learning. They need reasons to make a long-term memory commitment (rather than a commitment for one test). Seeing field situations can create their need to learn.

Developing printed schedules is good old-fashioned hard work. You must seek commitments from the work groups to support the schedule. Just as the work groups participated with you in developing the curriculum, they must cooperate in developing and supporting a training schedule. Here are some ways to promote that cooperation:

- Know your capabilities and flexibilities. When can specific training be offered, and when can it not be offered?

- Maintain close working relationships with work group supervisors.

- Meet face-to-face with groups, supervisors, and managers to iron out difficulties.

- Obtain the commitment of each work group to the training program, in writing. A procedure (chapter 4) describing the program is signed off by the work group supervisor. It becomes a contract. Breaches of that contract are reported to senior management. HRT is no-nonsense business.

- Obtain commitments as far in advance as possible. Work on a rolling schedule of at least twelve months. (In June of this year, you plan the schedule for June of next year.)

- Maintain a "canceled-training" file. Discover trends and discuss the trends with work group supervisors and senior management.

There are software programs that will assist in developing a schedule and tracking enrollment. Otherwise, you will need graph paper, rulers, and a big desk. Be sure to factor in the vacation times of your instructors and any planned down-time in the labs, shops, or simulator.

The next step is to publish the schedule. Trainees, supervisors, and instructors need to know what's coming. A well-designed schedule with enrollment information, phone numbers for information, and perhaps a map can be a vital communication link to all personnel. Although you may schedule a year in advance, you might not want to publish (hardcover or on mainframe for CRT access) a full year's schedule. Changes in extended schedules are hard to avoid. Consider a six-month schedule, published quarterly; you have to make sure the trainees and planners are aware of your routine and when you will deliver the curriculum.

## Delivery

Delivery, from a management view, is a matter of control, compliance, and safety. The right trainees, the right instructors and material, the right examinations, and the right records are the issues. Here is a good framework for several procedures.

*Right trainee.* A class enrollment is controlled. Enrollment occurs before a program begins and requires the work group supervisor's sign-off on an enrollment form. The form is sent to the training division where a preliminary roster is developed. All trainees' records are checked to ensure that they have not taken the course before, have had the prerequisite courses, and indeed need the course for their overall program (matrix completion).

Trainees who meet these requirements are contacted in writing (copy to supervisor) confirming enrollment and given the following information:

- When the course begins
- Where to meet for the first class
- Tools or equipment to bring (e.g., always bring identification)
- Preparation they should do before the class starts (e.g., read manual XX2)
- Duration of the course
- Meaning of the course to their career (or other motivating comments)
- If they will be traveling or living away from their domicile

All details for housing and transportation should be covered.

The correspondence should also include steps for the trainee to follow to cancel enrollment and phone numbers to call for additional information and in case of problems.

Once they arrive at the training site, there must be some way to direct the new trainees to the correct building or room. The solution might be as simple as a directory board at the entrance to the training center, a receptionist, or maps handed out at the main gate (receptionists and gate personnel must have adequate information). When trainees arrive in the correct room, verify identification and take an inventory of tools or equipment. Take steps to obtain items forgotten or not available to the trainees.

*Right instructors and training materials.* Even the most qualified instructor must have adequate preparation time to review for a course. Details must be refreshed. The right instructor means the most qualified, who also has the appropriate review time. Besides, people get sick, take vacations, have emergencies, and are often just overworked. Backup instructors are critical in the case of illness or personal problems.

Each program should have a course outline that provides the instructor with an inventory of all needed instructional materials such as each unit of instruction and all supporting instructional aids. All videotapes, transparencies, audiotapes, and so forth must be reviewed before a course begins to ensure proper condition for use.

Based on the roster, the appropriate number of copies of units of instruction are made and assembled for trainees. Usually they are placed in three-ring binders, in correct order. Other material to be included might be name tags, notepaper, and pencils. For a course that lasts more than a day, a training schedule should be enclosed.

*Right examinations.* Capabilities on generating tests vary. In the simplified situation, there is one version of an examination drawn from the test files, copied, and handed out. In the most complex situation, a computerized test bank creates an individual test for each person (all the same concepts are tested, but with variations on the questions). Somewhere in between is a course with three variations of the same test.

The instructor obtains the master test(s) and reads over the test(s) to see if some questions may be ambiguous because of the way the content was taught. If so, and with agreement with training supervisors, the ambiguous questions may be reworded or removed. Appropriate notes are placed in the test file to justify the action.

The instructor, or another appointed individual, provides security for the transportation of the test to the copying area, the copying of the test, and the destroying of any bad copies. The instructor returns the master to the files and receives a receipt. The instructor then checks the pages and serial numbers of the tests.

Before the test is administered, trainees' identities must again be verified. After the exam, the trainees are typically asked to sign a statement on the cover sheet that they neither gave nor received answers during the examination.

*Right records.* Following the HRT approach, the roster with test scores is signed off by the instructor and delivered to Records. Each individual examination is delivered to Records along with the completed answer sheet. Then, you disseminate the test results in accordance with procedures.

Training supervisors have the responsibility to monitor curriculum delivery. Catching a mistake before it becomes a problem is much easier than attempting to correct events later. Do not become discouraged when glitches occur in curriculum utilization. It takes longer to fine-tune a Jaguar than a Yugo.

Curriculum utilization means putting your product to work. All training staff members must be alert at all times, however, to ensure that the curriculum is properly used and improved. They must do so at each step in the utilization process of organizing, packaging, scheduling, and delivering the curriculum. Curriculum is a product that cannot stand alone. Your staff must nurture it.

# 7
# Utilizing Staff

A well selected and developed HRT staff can be compared to energy at rest. The potential for efficiency and effectiveness exists. All that is needed for productivity is a way to release the energy and direct it at achievable goals—staff utilization.

This chapter presents ways to encourage and allow the staff to competently perform. You need to know where the training group fits in the overall organization, some tips on the size and job functions of the staff, options on the structure of the training organization, how to develop productive planning methods that work in training, and ways to implement work plans.

## Where Training Fits into the Organization

Formal work organizations do three things when faced with major problems: reorganize, restaff, and retrain. As a result, HRT groups can be found at almost every level in organizations. In one sense, whether training is on the top tier, the bottom tier, or somewhere in between doesn't matter. If the organization believes in training, the function will be used and supported. If it doesn't, it won't.

The people who fill the top job positions (and allocate resources) often change. This reality requires a proximity of training to those positions. Training must be where it has the visibility and opportunity to educate senior decision makers— who may be new to their jobs—about the benefits of training and lobby for resources. Otherwise, you will have greater difficulty showing them that training makes effective use of resources. Face-to-face contact is the best way. Thus, the first rule:

> *Rule 1*: Training must have sufficient hierarchical status to report directly to the job position that allocates resources.

The next two rules deal with the role of training in organizational planning. Most organizations usually have three levels of planning: long-range, strategic, and tactical. Training has little need to be involved in the first; long-range planning usually concerns trends and forecasts, and what the organization might do in varying situations.

Training has, however, a definite role in strategic planning. Line managers meet and decide what is really going to happen over the next year (or longer). Training has in fact two roles. The first is to ensure that strategic planning takes into account the time required for and the cost of training. The other is to provide sound advice on planned purchases of hardware and software, such as, "No one has the background to repair that equipment; we will need specialized vendor training" or "How that black box works is proprietary information. Will they sell us the information, or are we stuck forever with their maintenance?" Thus, the second rule:

> *Rule 2*: Training must have sufficient hierarchical status to be on an even level with the line managers who make strategic decisions.

The tactical level of planning is done in each work group, where employees figure out how to carry out their assignment. Training's role is to advise the group on how much time training will take and to assist them in scheduling. Thus, the third rule:

Rule 3: Training must have sufficient hierarchical status to be a respected advisor to the work groups' planning.

The most important consideration in determining the location of HRT is that training must be a part of the system of checks and balances. Training must be able to say no to putting an operation in place before the people are thoroughly trained. Many pressures fall on operations personnel to get work accomplished and projects in place. The organization needs to use training in a checks-and-balances manner to protect itself and workers. Thus, the fourth rule:

Rule 4: Training must have sufficient hierarchical authority to delay the implementation of an operational work order.

These four rules are flexible enough to be applied in most organizations. Each organization is capable of coming up with other rules unique to specific situations.

## Staffing Tips

If you know how much training has to be delivered to how many trainees, and how often, you can use the following benchmarks:

- Instructors in highly technical areas with rapidly changing content can teach up to 50 percent of their work time (35–50 percent).

- Instructors in highly repetitive areas with slowly changing content can teach up to 75 percent of their work time.

- Straight lecture classes can be of any size.

- Lecture and discussion classes work best with 12–20 trainees.

- Labs and shops should rarely be more than 12 trainees.

- Initial simulator training must be one-to-one. Retraining can have a higher trainer-instructor ratio.

- One CBT proctor can handle up to 12 stations.

- You need one clerical position—performing word processing and records input and retrieval—for every two instructors.

- Add one working supervisor for every four employees.

All these positions need support. Instructors need curriculum development, job analysis, and test and measurements support. The simulators (firing range, mock operating room) require "as needed" support—there are no guidelines. Hardware and software support needs will vary depending on how well your simulator matches the real environment. A CBT development program and an off-the-shelf delivery program are vastly different. Audiovisual support can be simple, such as "Move the equipment around, and keep it running" or a full TV studio. Although no rules exist, there are some concerns to keep in mind:

- The support side of a training staff has the eerie habit of reflecting the background of the training manager or the trends of the year. Fads and likes and dislikes don't get you anywhere. A strong resource allocation to a video lab should only be made when a sizeable portion of the curriculum can be presented better on video than in less costly ways. CBT has to pay its own way in reducing trainee or instructor time.

- In HRT functions where the instructors cycle in and out on a rotating basis (e.g., the military, law enforcement), a strong support staff of professionals is required to ensure a consistent organization. The key person in such a transitory setting is the curriculum development supervisor.

- Simulators and part-task simulators are no better than their fidelity. Adequate software and hardware support is a safety necessity.

- Trainees and instructors alike require a collection of current procedures, research reports, textbooks, and microform information. An updated technical library will save money in research time.

- Software support for the records system, job analysis, test banks, and so forth need not be in-house but must be available.

These benchmarks, rules of thumb, ratios, and tips can help you. Even when you don't know the total training load, they provide some assistance. A training function can only be in one of three states: growing, level, or decreasing. In a growing or decreasing organization, you take your best conservative estimate and backfill with temporary personnel and consultants, saving money and pain. You have to make sure that the consultants eventually go away; otherwise, you will never have a stable organization.

## Training Organizational Structure

People expect organizations to work right. Most organizations have problems. So, structures are continually being changed. There are five reasons why formal work organizations never meet our expectations. These five are, if you will, built-in design flaws:

1. Organizational tasks are distributed among job positions. This division of labor is supposed to promote specialization, which is supposed to lead to expertise. In fact, however, employees with greater rather than less flexibility are desirable.

2. Job positions are structured into a hierarchical authority structure, usually in a pyramid form. The idea is that each person in a position is best qualified to make correct decisions about the work of those below. But the continual battle is, Who makes the decision: the technical expert or the hierarchical authority?

3. A formal system of rules and regulations ensures consistency in operation and provides for continuity when personnel change. Problems arise with bad rules and exceptions to rules.

4. Job holders are expected to have an impersonal orientation to all employees and clients. Everyone is supposed to be treated the same. This attitude denies the realities of interpersonal behavior.

5. Employment is considered a lifelong career. In fact, of course, most people change employment several times in the course of their work life.

There is a backfire, dysfunction, to each one of these faulty premises that can upset the equilibrium of an organization.

Too often, when faced with these built-in problems, leaders rush out to change the organizational structure. Although such action is no cure-all, beginning with a solid structure is nevertheless the first step to proper staff utilization. No one has invented an organization that beats all five design flaws. Yet, the problems can be minimized.

Figure 20 presents three popular models for an HRT function. None of these models is wrong. Each type can be found in every organizational environment. The so-called military model is tall, several layers. The business model is flat; everyone runs to the manager. The college model is in between, but suffers from two "camps" competing for resources.

Consider for a moment what you are really doing when you structure an organization:

- Assigning status to positions and groups

- Deciding how the authority will flow

- Describing a route for the distribution of resources

- Identifying the points of accountability

- Building an appeals route for grievances

These elements affect a part of the work efficiency of an organization, but just a part. When job positions in an HRT group are organized along the classical lines of job specialization (or rank or degrees), efficiency will suffer. Job specialization is not clearly dividable in HRT. Consider a "work functional" structure to obtain the goal of efficiency (see figure 21).

The only reason to have HRT is to develop, deliver, evaluate, and record a curriculum. You must strike for efficiency by organizing around the only reason HRT exists: the curriculum. Consider the structure in figure 22. It works, because it fits

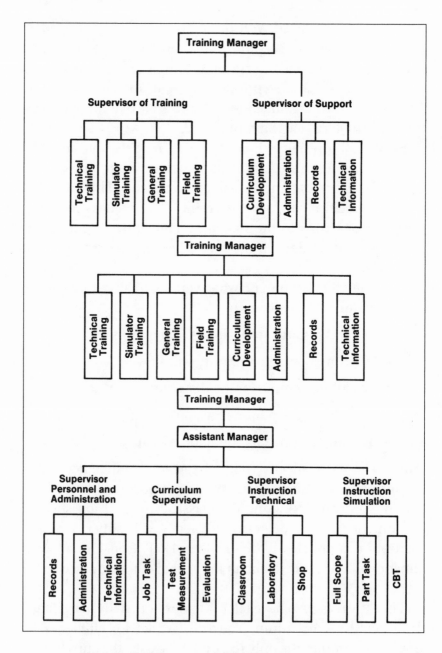

Figure 20.  Three traditional organizational structures.

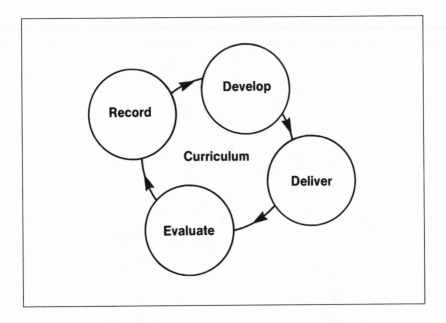

Figure 21. Conceptual organizational areas in training.

the needs. Depending on your situation, you may be justified in adding a fourth block in the second level for a supervisor of maintenance and services. There is never justification for adding an assistant to the manager. An "assistant to" either becomes a high-paid clerk or runs the organization. Either way, you have weak management. Let's examine the possibilities of each functional section.

In the *curriculum and instruction* section, the curriculum subsection may not even have permanent professional positions assigned beyond the supervisor and perhaps a job analysis specialist. Personnel are drawn from the instructional ranks for projects. Expertise applied and belief by the instructors in the final curriculum are the payoffs. The supervisor can also oversee all units of instruction and simulator scenario development. Major clerical support is placed where it belongs, generating curriculum on paper.

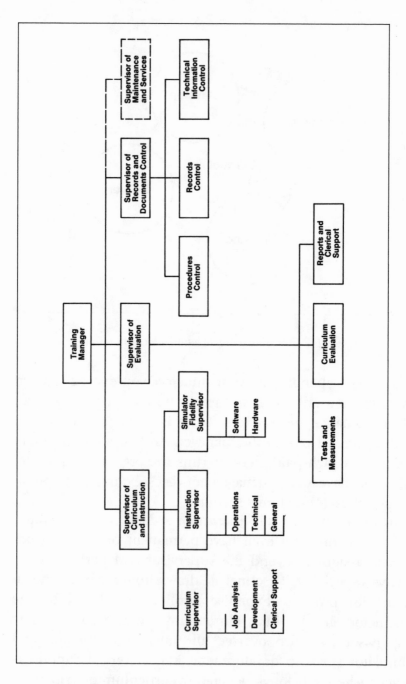

Figure 22. Optimal HRT organizational structure.

The instruction subsection is where the rubber hits the road. The supervisor can concentrate on effective training. The supervisor knows the materials are solid and can dig into the most effective ways to help the trainees learn the curriculum.

The simulator subsection has one purpose. It's clearly stated in the title: fidelity. The software and hardware people are part of the team and have the instructors' expertise handy to them without bureaucratic nonsense.

The *evaluation* section is the quality control system. For checks and balances, it must be separated. Having a compartment, a division, a different camp in the organization for evaluation is beneficial in HRT. The three subsections—tests and measurements, curriculum evaluation, and reports and clerical support—are functional in nature. Your situation will dictate the number of positions required and whether supervisors are needed. The tests and measurements subsection zeroes in on trainee evaluations—written tests, simulator evaluation forms, OJT report forms, field simulation evaluation forms—and how they are carried out. Even a valid and reliable evaluation is dangerous if implemented incorrectly.

The curriculum evaluation subsection is directly concerned with how well the curriculum moved the trainees to where they needed to be and how well the training was implemented on the job. The main evaluation tools include work performance observations, follow-up surveys with trainees and their supervisors, and comparisons to other organizations (How well do their physicians, pilots, officers, or operators do in comparison to ours?).

The records and clerical support personnel prepare survey forms, handle distribution and collection, and tabulate the data. After analysis, the group types and distributes reports.

In the records and documents control section, the thrust is the management of information. Procedures control is the management of the development, distribution, and updating of the controlling procedures (chapters 4, 8, and 12). Records control is the development, storage, retrieval, and distribution of training data (chapters 5, 9, and 13). Technical information control is another phrase for a technical library. Instructors must have the most current research and controlled information organized for their unique needs.

This organization is required for an HRT operation. Far from perfect, it comes closer to doing what an organization should do and reducing the traditional backfires. The only problem with a good organization chart is that the minute you "people" it, personalities come into play, and it may no longer seem like a good organization. There is a way out.

## Promoting Productivity

Think about a job position as shown on an organization chart. It's a box. Into that box are stuffed job requirements and a person. Someone with unique skills, abilities, and needs. Figure 23 shows the situation. The better the job requirements match the skills and abilities of the incumbent, the higher the efficiency, effectiveness, morale, and productivity. Morale is not how often people smile, frown, or grumble; morale is the outcome of the match between job requirements and the individual. How well the dual track converges determines the quality of work.

An individual is shaped by many factors. A whole group of factors fits under the psychosocial background label—how raised, where, values inculcated, and so forth. The individual has a trail of educational and work experiences. Each individual also comes with a unique set of personal needs such as health, safety, reward, contribution, status, and happiness.

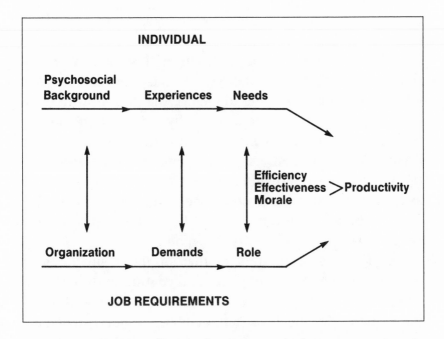

Figure 23. The match between job and individual.

On the other line in figure 23 you have the requirements of the job. The organization exists for a purpose. To accomplish that purpose, it places specific demands in the form of job descriptions. The description is translated into action, a role.

How does the concept illustrated in figure 23 help you with your dilemma (that people mess up a good organization chart)? It tells you, for example, that you don't place a person with strong religious beliefs of not harming fellow human beings in a combat organization. You don't place someone whose educational and work experience was in engineering in a job that demands direct health care of patients. The principle is to match the individual's psychosocial background with the organization, experiences with job demands.

By and large, we do a reasonably fair job in making these two matches.

We tend, however, to be less than impressive in matching the needs of an individual to the role. The process is a continual conflict of trying to change the person or the role or both. Billions are spent annually on solutions to the problem. Fad theories come and go, and new management training seminars (here, learn this system) are always sprouting up. We want each individual to be innovative but do exactly as expected. The game is unwinnable with some exceptions. In a think-tank, innovation is the demand. On an assembly line, workers must be exactly like robots.

An HRT organization is neither of those situations. It requires tremendous consistency and continuous innovation. It is an ideal situation to accommodate the unique needs of individuals. Allowing HRT staff members to spend 10 percent of their total time on the job performing work that meets their individual needs and interests can produce real dividends. The work gets done, while individual needs are met, and everyone gets the chance to grow—quite an achievement. It requires planning.

## Planning Work

To utilize your staff well, you must identify work outcomes and how the outcomes will be reached. There are three areas of consideration:

- HRT is a service organization. It's not the driving gear, it's the driven gear. This situation is managed by Planning Activities around Critical Events (PACE).

- Subsections and individuals must know the blocks of work they are expected to perform. This situation is managed by Management By Results (MBR).

- Individual work plans and innovation are required for the productivity and health of the organization and the morale of the individual. This situation is managed by Management By Objectives (MBO).

The major planning mistake made in a grass-roots HRT organization is to approach planning in increments of a one-year budget cycle. Plans and budgets must certainly go hand-in-hand; a budget is the way you carry out a plan. But circumstances change, and budgets (tools) must respond. Let's suppose you begin a new budget cycle every January. The development of that budget may have begun four to six months earlier. You are essentially forecasting eighteen months into the future. Good luck.

The reality is that your staff can be better utilized if you work with a twelve-month rolling plan and articulate the budget to your needs. Although you will have to submit an annual budget, your plan is more efficiently managed if each month you work one year ahead. That is, in April of this year, you are planning April of next year. (Also, you readjust each current month as you approach and go through the month.)

This approach can be done, but it requires an overall organization that can make the budget work productively for HRT, not for the bean-counters. Functional budget is the phrase, and the place to begin is by establishing planning parameters. They are required for the proper use of PACE, MBR, and MBO. A planning parameter is simply a statement that delineates scope of responsibility. Here are some examples:

- The Training Center is responsible for all training.

- The Training Center is responsible for all initial and advancement training.

- The Training Center is responsible for retraining, continuing training, and emergency training.

You can elaborate to enhance the bare-bones phrases, as in—

The Training Center is responsible to transmit to all personnel the values, knowledges, and skills necessary to ensure the safe and efficient operation of. . . .

The purpose is to establish the scope of responsibility, and your statement must pyramid down the organization chart.

- The curriculum and instruction group develops and delivers all on-site training and contracts all off-site training.

- The evaluation group continually monitors and periodically reports on all on-site training.

- The records and documents control group collects, stores, and retrieves all curriculum materials and trainees' records and collects and maintains a technical library.

The next step involves the scheduling of critical events for the PACE system. You must first identify the major driving events of a rolling one-year period, such as—

- For the programs for each type of training, initial, continuing, retraining, and advancement—when, where, how many trainees, how often?

- Emergency drills—when, what disciplines?

- Audits—when or how many annually?

- Others—elements unique to your organization.

Lay out these requirements on a planning calendar, noting the time needed for preparation, conduct, recording, and evaluation for each event (see figure 24).

You then translate the activities into work-block statements using an MBR format. Let's take the Sat-Tech Program–Level I as an example. You study the demands of the workload and figure out that you need three instructors (based on the 50 percent rule), one records clerk, and one evaluation specialist. You estimate that the instructors will need four weeks' preparation time, the records clerk will need two weeks to enter data, and the initial evaluation will take one week. The MBR could read in the following manner:

- Conduct Sat-Tech Program–Level I for twelve trainees between February 15 and May 15. Instructor prep is twelve instructor weeks, class time is thirty-six instructor weeks, records is two weeks, and evaluation is one week.

The next step is to develop individual work plans by a parallel MBO system (follows figure 23). Let's take as an

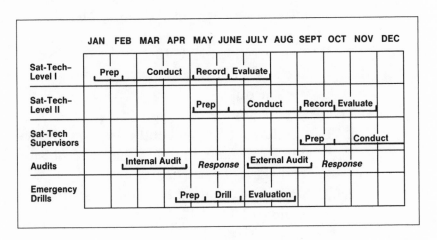

Figure 24. Example of a planning calendar.

example one instructor in the sat-tech program who also has other duties. There are three steps in the MBO process:

1. *List major blocks of work.* (Job analysis is covered in chapter 2.)

   1.1  Job - Instructor

   1.2  Major Blocks

       1.2.1  Curriculum Development

       1.2.2  Instructional Materials Development

       1.2.3  Instruction

       1.2.4  Trainee Evaluation

       1.2.5  Records Input

       1.2.6  Professional Development

       1.2.7  Innovation

2. *Assign measurable work objectives* in a face-to-face meeting with the instructor.

   2.1  Curriculum Development

       2.1.1  Review job analysis for Sat-Tech–Level I by March 1.

   2.2  Instructional Materials Development

       2.2.1  Revise and obtain approval of instructional material for Sat-Tech–Level I by March 15.

   2.3  Instruction

       2.3.1  Teach sections 13.1, 13.2, and 13.6 of Sat-Tech–Level I between March 15 and July 15 per schedule.

   2.4  Trainee Evaluation

       2.4.1  Conduct interim and end-of-section evaluation for sections 13.1, 13.2, and 13.6 of Sat-Tech–Level I per schedule.

       2.4.2  Observe and judge field simulation trials on section 13.9.

2.5 Records

    2.5.1 Transmit updated and approved instructional materials on Sat-Tech–Level I to Records before instruction begins for each section.

2.6 Professional Development

    2.6.1 Complete advanced instructor certification by September 15.

    2.6.2 Attend Microwave Conference November 12–16.

2.7 Innovation (This block is for the individual. In it, objectives designed to meet individual needs, interests, and abilities can be written. In a sense, you and the individual make a contract that binds the person to try something new, and the organization to support the effort with resources.) Here are some examples:

    2.7.X Research, develop, and deliver a paper to the training staff on methods of streamlining the curriculum revision process by August 1.

    2.7.Y Create a videotape on micromill radar functioning by September 15.

    2.7.Z Develop a safety plan for the training center by November 15.

3. *Hold monthly meetings*, face-to-face, between the supervisor and the individual to review progress and to establish the next month's (one-year hence) work is the final and continuing step.

The rolling MBO system saves time in giving work directions. One formal meeting a month keeps each party alert, allows for changes, and keeps each staff member directed at the work requirements. Its orientation to the future puts a training staff on the cutting edge of sound management.

The use of PACE and the recognition that training is driven by critical events is the key conceptual step. MBR packages the work into planning blocks. MBO gives specific directions to each staff member and allows some portion of the work to be individualized.

Staff utilization begins with organizing a functional set of tiers that matches the needs of training. You can get ahead in the management struggle if you recognize the dysfunctional aspects of organizations. Remember, too, that the systematic flow of work directions to each individual in a clear and concise manner increases the efficiency, effectiveness, morale, and productivity of the group. In HRT, having an effective staff is not simply a desirable management goal. It is critical. How well your staff does what it does can mean the difference between life and death.

# 8
# Utilizing Procedures

Procedures are part of the communication system that links the HRT function to the rest of the organizaiton. Internally, procedures are day-to-day tools to be used by the staff. The ultimate purpose of procedures is to cause consistency in behavior. Consistency is the way you guarantee your input to the eventual safe and efficient work of those who complete training.

This chapter presents ways to utilize procedures. You will need to know how to orient new staff members, inform the staff of changes and additions, enforce the use of procedures, and deal with requests for exceptions to procedures.

## Staff Orientation

New HRT staff members must learn both internal and external procedures. New supervisors outside of training, who have responsibilities to training, are responsible for learning the external procedures. One of the most common mistakes in providing orientation to new personnel is to have a sit-down talk-through of all procedures within the first few days on the new job. The only thing worse is to toss them the manuals and walk away.

The first few weeks on a new job are the honeymoon stage. Next comes the make-it or break-it stage. If the new staff member survives, the continuing stage is, one hopes, a steady-state operation (as steady as any operation can be). The honeymoon stage is filled with excitement, confusion, and attempts to learn the job. Things learned during this stage tend to be only surface-level learning. The person has yet to face a problem. Adults are problem-based learners. With so much going on, you can expect that an overview of training procedures will be lost in the shuffle. Procedure orientation is a timing issue.

The second issue concerns the nature and background of the new staff member. You have to make some assumptions and do some classifying. There are at least three reasons procedures are not followed:

- Personnel are unaware the procedure exists.

- The procedure is subverted because it is filled with needless barriers that retard work.

- Personnel make a conscious decision to ignore the procedure.

What might be the nature and background of a person who would decide to ignore a procedure? Highly educated professionals seem to have a natural disdain for following directions. This observation is particularly true when the professionals come from a background that seemed procedureless. They have to be educated on the philosophy and role of procedures. The education must occur before specific procedures are taught or can be learned.

Who else might fall into this category? How about people with inflated egos? Arrogance will not allow them to be subservient to a piece of paper. They are essentially showing off. Perhaps they like to ride near the edge and get a thrill from ignoring the rules. They, too, require an indoctrination on the value of procedures and supervisory monitoring. These two types require a different orientation treatment.

What kind of a person would subvert a procedure because it is filled with needless barriers? Almost anyone. New staff members may bring a fresh view and see other ways to accomplish work. Therefore, the orientation is not only on the meat of the procedures, but on how procedures are developed and changed. The orientation might include a mandate to make the procedures more effective and give specific steps to take when faced with an unwieldy procedure.

An overview of the entire procedure system is required to ensure that new staff members are aware of all procedures. For, some procedures outside the training system, such as personnel administration procedures, may affect training. Knowing how all procedures are indexed is a vital part of the orientation.

The third issue is one of technical languages in procedures. Every industry and profession has its own language. The acronyms, technical slang, and abbreviations may take a considerable time to learn. In some cases, the language is easier to teach to persons who are naive than persons coming from peer organizations. The latter may think they already know the jargon. They are at risk because there are always subtle differences and sometimes major differences. So, the procedure orientation must include a language lesson, and where to go for help in interpretation.

In sum, the three issues of an orientation to procedures for new staff are:

- Timing of the orientation
- Nature and background of new staff
- Knowledge of the technical language

Meeting the issues correctly is time consuming, but it will pay off in the long run. The following tips will help:

- Have an initial orientation during the honeymoon stage: "We have procedures. We have them because. . . . Here is how the system works. Become acquainted with the titles. My telephone number is. . . ."

- Have a second orientation after the honeymoon period, when the new employee is faced with problems. Get into the meat of the procedures. Provide as much assistance on the technical language as possible.

- Monitor the new staff member closely during the honeymoon stage. Be an over-the-shoulder supervisor.

- During the make-it or break-it stage, be supportive and firm. Meet noncompliance head-on. In this stage, the most rapid learning is experienced with the best retention rate.

- Shepherd the new employee through a procedure rewrite. This experience promotes an undersanding, appreciation, and a respect for the procedure system.

By this time, the new staff member is getting used to the organization. Like all staff members, he or she must be kept up to date on all changes and additions to the system.

## Communicating Changes and Additions

Procedures change as technology, methods, and incumbents change. The key is redundancy in written and oral communications. The following strategies will help:

*Written communication.* The first notification of a procedural change must come from the procedure development and sign-off system. Build in a routine step that requires the issuance of a change notice to all training staff members (whether manual holders or not) and all external manual holders. The change notice should be short and to the point. The core of the message must be how the change affects the way the staff does business. Other written means include memos, newsletters, and posting notices on bulletins boards.

*Oral communication.* You have only two choices: staff meetings and one-to-one conversations. Use the staff meeting to announce and reinforce. Use one-to-one conversations to ascertain individual awareness of changes.

## Enforcing Use of Procedures

To obtain the uniform use of procedures you almost certainly will eventually have to force compliance. Training, education, indoctrination, and assistance will sometimes fall short of the mark. Staff members are not necessarily trying to purposely subvert the system; many factors can cause a failure.

Enforcement is a matter of having checkpoints that you monitor for compliance. The format of your procedures should establish the checkpoints. A common method is to work from the end back through the system to determine if and where compliance may have derailed or been incomplete. That process essentially requires pulling the completed procedure forms from records and tracing them back. It works only if forms were submitted. All that can really be established by working backward through the system is to identify mistakes of omission or commission. It won't tell you why.

A more supervisory approach is to interject yourself in the midst of a process and investigate compliance in a business-like fashion. You can only discover two things: compliance or noncompliance. In the case of noncompliance, there are two reasons: purposeful or nonpurposeful. Both require actions. Nonpurposeful noncompliance may be traced to a system problem or lack of knowledge by a staff member. Purposeful noncompliance may be a sign (albeit an incorrect one) of a poor procedure. Repeated purposeful noncompliance by a staff member should result in an escalating series of supervisory actions, beginning with counseling. Persistent noncompliance should result in the application of sanctions with the final step being termination. Procedures in HRT are serious business. So is making exceptions.

## Making Exceptions to Procedures

A continuous management activity in any organization is dealing with requests for exceptions to rules. The more procedures in place, the higher the number of requests. Exceptions violate the "everyone treated the same" principle of organizations. There are occasions when exceptions must occur. It is usually a timing issue. Here are some guidelines on approving exceptions:

- Every exception granted will come back to haunt you: "You did it for so-and-so." Each exception must be accompanied by documentation of extenuating and mitigating circumstances. The documentation becomes a part of the records. When others request exceptions, you must inform them of the conditions under which previous exceptions were granted.

- Repeated requests for an exception to the same rule or step in a procedure may point out a problem with the procedure. A reexamination of the procedure is in order.

- Repeated requests by one staff person for exceptions to various procedures may point out an employee problem that requires supervisory attention.

Procedures cannot be allowed to stop an organization from functioning. Flexibility can be built into procedures. Alternative routes should be allowed if safety is not an issue. Overall, frequent requests for exceptions may indicate a weak procedures system.

To make proper use of procedures requires training, education, indoctrination, monitoring, and enforcement. A continual managerial awareness of the use and misuse of procedures is essential for success. Procedures must be flexible but still provide control.

# 9
# Utilizing Records

A records function is the official working system for depositing and retrieving information. Beyond the traditional uses, you have the opportunity to make the information productive, or at least have it become a source of energy to make things happen.

This chapter presents ways to utilize records. You need to understand the potential uses of information, traditional uses of records, the functions of performance indicators, planning performance indicators, packaging performance indicators, and how to design performance indicator distribution strategies.

## What Data Can Do for You

There is no need to store information unless you need to retrieve it; there is no need to retrieve information unless you're going to use it, and use it to make something happen. There is more to records systems than a computer.

A computer is to information as a power generating station is to an electrical system. The electricity is of no use unless it runs machines, provides lights, and keeps people warm.

The information coming from a records system is like energy. How the energy is used determines its productivity (or contribution to productivity). We don't always understand information. For much of the history of the world, people saw no use for coal, oil, and waterfalls. Information is too often viewed as something to avoid, "walk around," or simply to "stack up." Once we began to use fossil fuel for energy, we found it had other uses: nylon, plastic, and pharmaceuticals. The parallel to a records system is that beyond the traditional uses of records, there are ways to squeeze out additional uses, to exploit the records for additional productivity.

Nevertheless, traditional use precedes exploitation.

## Traditional Uses of Records

Chapter 5 noted three purposes for valid data: conducting day-to-day business operations, conducting training center business, and providing a data base for investigative reasons. Under those three headings, the following uses are traditional.

*Trainee status.* These data are used by the work groups in the decision process for job assignments, performance appraisals, promotions, job transfers, and in determining licensure and certification status. The data are used by training personnel for scheduling, counseling, admission to classes and programs, and follow-up evaluations.

The frequency the data are needed depends on the user. In some organizations, where employees must be trained and qualified on various pieces of hardware and programs before work can occur, the job planner may be the most frequent user.

Work groups, supervisors, and trainees need at least quarterly reports. In the case of licensure and certification, a red-flag system must be built into the records program that alerts employees and supervisors.

*Planning data.* Planning is simply a matter of knowing where you are, where you are going, and how to achieve that difference. Budgeting is applying a cost to that difference. The records system can tell you where you are. If built around the matrix approach (where every trainee has an end goal, chapter 5), it can then tell you where you are going. The linking of costs to services (as described in chapter 5) makes budget preparation a routine function.

*Audits and investigations.* The records system is the base for audits and investigations. There are two points to consider. One, be an auditor too. Conduct your own internal audits on procedure compliance frequently. During those audits, look at your system as an outsider would. That attitude will lead to improvements. Two, make sure the records system is procedurally based, not "person-based." If a records system can only be accessed by one person, you have a significant problem.

Another traditional use of data, end-of-year reports—dull, dry columns of numbers—is typical in formal organizations. Tables of numbers are needed, but annual statistical reports do not serve as a source of energy, a way to get records to affect productivity by making things happen.

To make information more productive means extracting more uses than merely the traditional. One way to accomplish the stretching required for productivity of data is to create performance indicators.

## Functions of Performance Indicators

Performance indicators (PIs) are representations of data that present evidence of movement toward goals, or lack of movement, or failure. PIs are more than internal public relations efforts. They are a way to present the training function in a capsulized form. The purposes of presenting training in such a format are:

- To give work groups meaningful "pictures" of their progress toward completing training commitments

- To allow training personnel to recognize their achievements and the quantity of work remaining

- To show senior decision makers the productivity of training and the flow of resources required

- To give other parties (boards, advisory groups, media) an appreciation of the training effort

PIs are not one-shot presentations. PIs are periodically issued visual communication links that track progress toward predetermined ends. Usually a PI presents baseline data, gives a current benchmark, and shows an explicit end. Figure 25 is an example.

The work group supervisor of the sat-techs, by reviewing figure 25, has a one-page opportunity to understand the training requirements. A back-up chart or phone call to Records can add specifics. The one page becomes a motivator for the work group supervisor to plan and request resources. It also provides senior decision makers with a barometer of work force qualifications and a starting point to discuss a work group's progress—or lack of progress—toward full qualification.

PIs, as a formal means of communication, require in-depth planning. There seems to be a hidden rule in planning communications. The shorter the message, the longer the planning time.

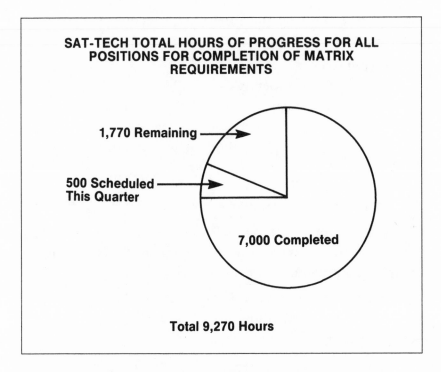

**SAT-TECH TOTAL HOURS OF PROGRESS FOR ALL POSITIONS FOR COMPLETION OF MATRIX REQUIREMENTS**

1,770 Remaining

500 Scheduled This Quarter

7,000 Completed

**Total 9,270 Hours**

Figure 25. Sample performance indicator.

## Planning Performance Indicators

Several planning factors are involved in creating PIs. There is not an exact order to the planning process. Although some steps obviously precede others, many can be accomplished at the same time. Let's take each factor independently, then weave everything together.

PIs are "reporting points" in tracking systems. One of the first decisions is deciding what you want and need to track. There are many elements to consider, but begin with some communication goals such as, "Whom do you want to know what?" You establish the goals by identifying the population with whom you desire to communicate and matrixing that list with the tracking potential of the records system. The populations are easy to identify:

- Trainees
- Work group supervisors
- Senior managers
- Boards and other parts of the organization
- Media, general population, specific public constituencies
- Training staff
- Training management

Identifying the tracking potential of the records is less simple. There are three ways to approach the classifying of the tracking potential:

1. *Types of data approach.* There are five broad types of data: curriculum, staff, evaluation, cost, and records.

2. *Work activities approach.* View the tracking systems as having three categories: ingredients, processes, and outcomes. The ingredients include curriculum, staff, money, facilities, and equipment. Processes include delivery of instruction and the records function. Outcomes include evaluations, achievement of license, certification, number of trainees completing training, etc.

3. *Selective perception.* Another name for this area is "What's handy?" It indeed has some uses in checking out the acceptability of PIs to the populations. It can provide feedback on the merits of this type of communication with a minor investment of resources.

Let's work through some examples, using option 2, the work activities approach. It requires three groups of communication goal matrices, one group for each of the three categories of ingredients, processes, and outcomes. Each category requires several matrices. Three examples are given, but the potential number of matrices could be close to one hundred.

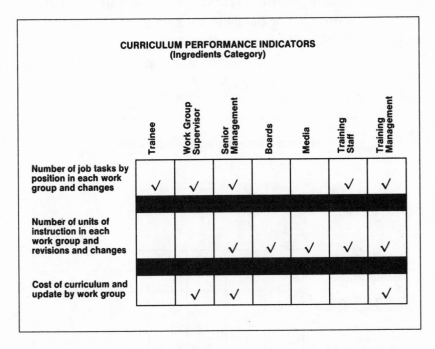

Figure 26. Example of a communication goal matrix using the ingredients category of tracking systems.

Each matrix (see figure 26) allows you to make a decision to set a communication goal. The top of each matrix is the same, a generic list of populations with whom you need to communicate. The list going down the left-hand side is drawn from the capabilities of your records system. As you work through the cells, you must decide if there is a worthwhile goal in communicating the information on the left to the listed populations. Dozens of other possibilities could be inserted along the left-hand margin; the emphasis is on the communication goal decision you make in each cell.

Study the matrix in figure 26. It lists information from the ingredients category. Is it indeed important for senior management to be aware of number of job tasks, units of instruction, changes and revisions? Yes. Absolutely! We make the assumption senior decision makers need to know about costs. They also need to know that the curriculum is keeping up with the times. They need to know how much work the training function is accomplishing.

| | Trainee | Work Group Supervisor | Senior Management | Boards | Media | Training Staff | Training Management |
|---|---|---|---|---|---|---|---|
| **TRAINING LOAD PERFORMANCE INDICATORS** | | | | | | | |
| Classroom utilization | | | | | | | ✓ |
| Simulator utilization | | | ✓ | | | | ✓ |
| Number of trainee contact hours by work group | ✓ | | | | | ✓ | ✓ |
| Average cost of training per contact hour by work group | ✓ | ✓ | ✓ | ✓ | ✓ | ✓ | ✓ |

Figure 27. Example of a communication goal matrix using the processes category of tracking systems.

Let's take another example. Figure 27 lists information from the processes category. Again, the same question is, "Whom do you want to know what?" Probably few other than training supervisors are going to regularly care about classroom utilization. But everyone should be concerned about average cost of trainee contact hours. "What is the message you want to get across?" is the other question. You might want to say—

- "We're working hard."
- "We're business-oriented."
- "We're short on funds."
- "We're expensive."
- "We're cheap."

What it really comes down to is, "Are you worth it?" Thus, figure 28 presents an example from the third category, outcomes.

| | Trainee | Work Group Supervisor | Senior Management | Boards | Media | Training Staff | Training Management |
|---|---|---|---|---|---|---|---|
| **OUTCOME PERFORMANCE INDICATORS** | | | | | | | |
| Percentage of training program completed by work group | | √ | √ | √ | | √ | √ |
| Number of potential trainees completing license and certification programs | | √ | √ | √ | √ | √ | √ |
| Number of audit findings compared to past | | | √ | √ | | √ | √ |

Figure 28. Example of a communication goal matrix using the outcomes category of tracking systems.

The list of performance indicators could become lengthy. One factor involved is the frequency of distribution. "Who needs what? How often?" A tip: work on monthly, quarterly, and annual PIs. Systems are easier to build in that fashion. Semiannual and biennial don't fit the ways most organizations do business.

One use of PIs is as a part of a budget presentation. Using the PIs to justify a budget is a tricky matter. PIs reflect a state of condition, and the interpretation of that state is in the eyes of the viewer. A training supervisor may see a PI as a workload forecast. A work group supervisor may see it as a hurdle to overcome while getting work done. A senior decision maker may see it as a needless cost or as the way to achieve excellence in the work force's productivity. Here are some strategies for getting senior decision makers to see the PIs as solid budget justification:

- *They must trust the data.* You must teach them— educate them—on how the data are collected, validated, and assembled. They must appreciate the integrity of the data.

- *They must want to cooperate with training.* Cooperation in formal organizations is achieved by communicating your purpose—over and over.

- *They must be able to interpret the data.* Formulating data is done with the distribution population in mind, not professionals in statistics.

**Packaging Performance Indicators**
There are two ways to package data: using the actual number in an organized table or converting the data to a graph. Figure 29 shows the same set of data presented in two different ways, a table and a graph—in this case, a bar graph. There is one rule: Each table or graph must stand alone. The title must clearly and concisely identify the contents. All necessary explanations must be on the chart. A paragraph is not needed

### MONTHLY TRAINING CENTER FACILITY UTILIZATION

| Space | Maximum Hours Available | Average Usage 5-Year Base | Current Month Usage |
|---|---|---|---|
| 10 Classrooms | 2,000 | 1,400 | 1,292 |
| 4 Labs | 800 | 560 | 613 |
| 1 Simulator | 200 | 140 | 121 |
| Total | 3,000 | 2,100 | 2,026 |

### MONTHLY TRAINING CENTER FACILITY UTILIZATION

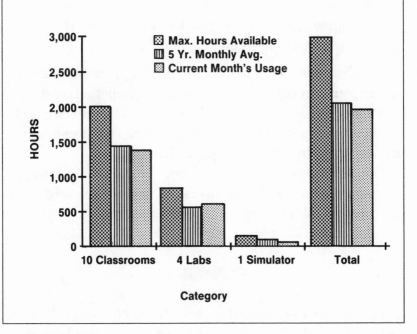

Figure 29. The same set of data presented in table form and graph form.

to explain the information per se, but may be needed to explain how the data may be interpreted or used. Tables often provide more information, but graphs are usually easier to assimilate. Graphs, despite losing detail, have a higher visual impact and retention rate. Another choice to be made is whether to use numbers or percentages. You will not be able to predict which persons take in data better in tabular form and which in graphic form. When you distribute graphs, therefore, you would do well to accompany them with detailed tables.

### Distributing Performance Indicators

There are three easy steps in the distribution of PIs:

- Tell people the PIs are coming.
- Distribute the PIs.
- Follow up to see if the PIs were received and respond to questions.

The distribution media include mailings, annual statistical reports, staff meetings, annual meetings, bulletin boards, and newsletters. The use of color graphs and 35-mm color slides add to the magnitude of the impact. Color slides should be accompanied by charts and paper handouts.

The follow-up scheme is basic business. Contact the opinion makers and the decision makers to help them interpret the information. You can use the time, too, to educate them about HRT.

The only reason to have a records system is to utilize the data. Beyond day-to-day business and investigative reasons, records can be used both to promote an understanding of training's contribution and to make things happen in resource allocation. Bear in mind that your data can work for you only if you present them in ways that people can understand and act on.

This chapter completes the implementation and utilization portion of HRT. These are two of the three rings you must balance. In Part 3, Evaluating, chapters 10 through 13 move you into the empirical world of evaluating your efforts to identify needed areas of change.

# Part 3:
# Evaluating

For too long, training has been considered a nebulous area of work where results could not be proven. Those days are gone. The technology of training provides a solid base from which empirical evidence can be collected and analyzed and then success or failure judged. Having developed the training function and implemented the programs, you *evaluate*—you find out how well the systems and people, including yourself, performed.

Beyond giving empirical measures of success or failure, evaluation results become the basis for modifying management systems. This group of chapters presents you with hands-on experience with the new thrust of evaluation methods. These evaluation methods take training out of some nebulous realm and put it on the same level as other organizational groups that must provide proof of production.

Chapter 10, Evaluating Curriculum, shows a firm method of curriculum evaluation and how to report to and deal with curriculum committees. It also teaches how to develop evaluation instruments. This skill is needed in the next chapters and in your work. Chapter 11, Evaluating Staff, gives a lesson on how to develop a philosophy of evaluation and ways to perform staff evaluations, and it presents the upscale approach of performance-anchored rating scales for trainers. The chapter closes with firm strategies on how to communicate evaluation results to staff members. Chapter 12, Evaluating Procedures, shows how to evaluate procedures by use of a communication cycle. You will also find the communication cycle helpful in other management duties. Chapter 13, Evaluating Records, essentially describes how to conduct an audit of a records system.

# 10
# Evaluating Curriculum

Curriculum evaluation focuses on deciding whether the race track you designed has the proper configuration to prepare completers for safe and efficient application of job tasks. A review of the two curriculum models in chapter 2 shows two points of evaluation: delivery (during the course of instruction) and work (job application).

This chapter presents ways to accomplish evaluations. You must understand the concept of evaluation, the scheme of an evaluation, data collection and measuring instrument development, and tips on judging data results with curriculum committee members.

## Curriculum Evaluation Scheme

The word evaluation is of French origin. It connotes action:

| EVALU | ATION |
|-------|-------|
| ↓ | ↓ |
| VALUE | STATE OF BEING |

In training, it means determining the value, or worth, of a curriculum in its current state of being. Evaluation is accomplished by measuring the curriculum at its point of delivery and at the point of application (on the job). Evaluation is further accomplished by the curriculum committee's judging the worth of the curriculum. The question to be answered by the curriculum committee is, "Should the curriculum remain the same or be altered?" To form a responsible answer to the question requires measurement and judgment in an organized fashion.

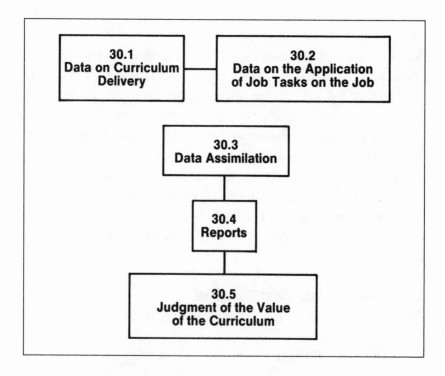

Figure 30. Curriculum evaluation scheme.

Figure 30 presents a linear scheme for conducting a curriculum evaluation. This approach fulfills the feedback loops described in the curriculum models in chapter 2. Each block in the evaluation scheme has some core elements. Your situation should add some unique elements. Let's go through the steps.

*Data on curriculum delivery (30.1).* You must measure how well the curriculum is ordered (Are the courses sequenced in the most effective manner?), how well the content is packaged (Is the simulator effective in this course?), and how well the trainees learned (How did the trainees perform on the end-of-course examination?).

*Data on the application of the job task on the job (30.2).* You must measure trainees' retention and ability to apply the learned content.

*Data assimilation (30.3).* This step is the locus point where the data are brought together (Everyone scored low in this course, and job application was low. What's wrong?). Some of the data may stand alone (End of course critique by trainees gave it low marks; but, their scores were high, and job application was good.).

*Reports (30.4).* This step is the mechanical process of putting the data into understandable reports. There is a specific format to the reports: show data, conclusions (what you think the data mean), and your recommendations. Showing the data allows others to double-check you and come up with some other ideas.

*Judgment of the value of the curriculum (30.5).* The curriculum committee uses group decision making to determine the worth of the curriculum in its current configuration (Is it the right race track, in the right place, packaged in the right manner?).

Never fall victim to a formula approach to curriculum evaluation (for example, if 22 percent of the trainees score below 80 on the end-of-course examination, then the course must be rewritten). There are too many variables in learning and curriculum to relegate a curriculum decision to mere statistical formulas. The data must be judged by people; that is true evaluation.

In helping the curriculum committee function in the evaluation stage, you will collect, or supervise the collection of, data. You're trying to take a picture, with data, of the true situation. There are rules to this type of photography.

## Data Collection and Measuring Instruments

Collecting data has the same purpose as taking a photograph. You want the picture to be as accurate a reflection of the real thing as possible (validity). You want the camera to deliver the same high-quality picture each time (reliability). You want the main subject clear, not fuzzy or overpowered by needless background (definition).

The first rule in data collection is to set the stage. You must *define what you're going to measure*, which gets everything else out of the background. If you were going to measure this book, a solid object you can see, you would give little thought to defining it; all you need is a tape measure, and it's done. Now, let's suppose you're going to measure something that's not a solid object, like the sequencing or packaging of courses in a curriculum. What do you want to know?

- Is the current arrangement adequate?
- Is the current packaging adequate?
- Is there a better way?

Well, there's always a better way, but that's the function of research. Your function in this mode is evaluation. After you've made the judgment (evaluated) that it's not good, then you move to research. Don't get caught up in research at this point.

This step is simply defining what you want to photograph.

For example—

- Is the sat-techs learning on basic nutrition from the CBT program adequate?

- Is the simulator course on in-space living correctly sequenced in the program?

- Does the pace of the curriculum match the learning abilities of the trainees?

Concise and specific as possible, each photograph stands alone at this point. The next issue is measurement. You must develop your own tape measure.

Measuring something unseeable is a matter of logic. Logic is based on assumptions. Your goal, and the second rule, is *reliable measurement*. Let's take a closer look at one of the evaluation questions:

- Is the sat-techs learning on basic nutrition from the CBT program adequate?

Don't worry about the word *adequate* at this point. How can you measure the trainees' learning? For starters, you have end-of-course test scores. You can average them and make a general statement that is useful to the curriculum committee.

You can also make the assumption that the trainees have opinions (both at the end of the course and when they return from their first space flight). The proctor in CBT should be able to communicate the difficulty or ease with which trainees moved through the class. (The computer will track the amount of time taken and how each trainee did on interim questions.) If the sat-techs return from space with vitamin deficiencies, you have another measure.

The point here is that one photo (end-of-class scores) is not adequate. You must take several pictures from several angles. Then you and the curriculum committee must judge "what is adequate." But, first, you have to record the measurements.

The third rule is to have *reliable recording devices*. Let's create some titles for block 30.1, data on curriculum delivery:

- Trainee end-of-course critique
- Instructor and proctor end-of-course critique
- End-of-course grade summary
- Retest rate per course
- Interview schedule for noncompleters

Let's make a comparison. Although a house can be any shape, it must have a foundation, a floor, walls, and a roof. Just like a house of any shape, a reliable recording device must have certain components to assist in achieving reliability:

- A heading or title that clearly places fences around the subject to be measured (Consider only this one course, no other courses.).

- Directions that clearly tell how to complete the form (Read each sentence and respond with only one check (✓) per sentence in the blocks to the right. Do not place checks between the blocks.).

- A measuring scale—for example, a one-to-five scale at the far right side of the page—that is simple for the completer and makes recording results on a summary sheet easy.

- Space for written comments by the completer.

- Space for the exact recording of the specific class, section, date, etc., and signature of completer.

- Clear indication of when the form is completed (e.g., END).

Some training organizations object to the signing of evaluation sheets by trainees. They fear the trainees will not be honest if required to sign. HRT is too important to work by high school rules. Get the signatures, and follow up if trainees' responses raise questions in your mind.

Figure 31 is an example of an end-of-course curriculum critique form to be completed by trainees. It measures the four concepts of pace (PA), packaging (PK), content (C), and placement (PL), with three questions on each concept. Some of the questions are redundant and asked in a reverse manner. The purpose of redundancy and reversal is to identify set responses (from people who just mark without reading) and remove those critiques from the valid stack.

Content questions are numbers 1, 5, and 9. Pace questions are numbers 2, 6, and 10. Placement questions are numbers 3, 7, and 11. Packaging questions are numbers 4, 8, and 12. Trainees are best qualified to respond to pace and packaging questions. They will have a sense of placement. They are least qualified to judge content, but they can tell you some things.

Figure 31 is an example of one measuring device. You will need to develop as many as required to cover all the angles of the subject you intend to accurately reflect for block 30.1.

Block 30.2, data on the application of job tasks on the job, is the next area requiring measurement. The measuring devices are easier to develop (use job analysis), but harder to collect (a follow-up program is required). The completers are on the job and no longer under your control in the training environment. There are two populations, at least, to contact: former trainees and their supervisors. There are three follow-up programs (using task analysis with a measuring scale) to collect the data: mailed surveys, interviews, and work observations.

END-OF-COURSE CURRICULUM CRITIQUE

COURSE: _____  _____  _____
                    Title                          Section          Dates (Beginning-End)

PURPOSE: The data reported on this form will assist in improving the curriculum. Your candid response
is needed.

DIRECTIONS: At the left are a series of phrases. Read each phrase. At the right of each phrase is a one
(1) to five (5) scale. Marking on the low end shows low agreement. Marking on the high end shows high
agreement. Place a check (√) under the number that matches your agreement. Do not place checks on
the lines between numbers. Make only one check per phrase. Do not leave any phrases unchecked.

                                                                    Low Agree   High Agree
                                                                    1   2   3   4   5

1. The tasks taught should be useful in my job.

2. The course was too fast.

3. The course fit in well with the other courses.

4. The ways used to teach the course (lecture, simulator, CBT) were
   good.

5. I will never use much of what was taught.

6. The content could have been covered more quickly.

7. I needed more background in this course.

8. Other ways of teaching this course should be considered.

9. I think everyone with whom I work should take this course.

10. The course was easy.

11. I think this course should be taught earlier or later in the program.

12. The course was not confusing.

Comments: _____
_____
_____
_____

Printed Name _____  Signature _____

Social Security Number _____  Date _____

END

Figure 31. Sample end-of-course critique form for trainees to complete.

It's good business to contact both populations and use all three methods of collecting data. For data that will be most useful to curriculum evaluation, conduct the follow-up between three and six months of program completion—time enough to apply many of the tasks, but not too long to forget where the skills were learned.

Three more rules about data collection before you begin a follow-up curriculum evaluation. They deal with cause and effect, confounding, and sampling.

*Cause and effect* means there is a direct relationship between the way an entity is treated and the entity's behavior. You heft a rock, you apply force by tossing it, and it flies through the air. You put trainees through a program, they go to the job, and. . .perhaps they perform as taught, perhaps not. Training is not a direct cause-and-effect system. The best you can hope for is *cause and affect*. A training program can no more take the total credit for an outstanding worker than it can for an outstanding failure. There are too many variables at work within and around each trainee. You can at best influence how a trainee will behave after training; you cannot guarantee it.

On-the-job measurements of curriculum must be collected and interpreted with an understanding of how things become *confounded*. If you intend to measure the amount of water you are sprinkling on your newly sodded lawn with a rain gauge and it rains, your results have been confounded. You know how much water the lawn received, but not its source. On the job, there are many factors that can confound how well former trainees perform, not the least of which are management systems and direct supervision.

*Sampling* is really a work aid to you. Given seven hundred job tasks, thirty-one completers and supervisors, and your limited input personnel and computing space, you don't want to manage that much data. And, you don't need it to arrive at valid conclusions. Using the job task analysis as a base, for curriculum evaluation purposes there are two types of samples: random and stratified.

In a random sample, you select tasks for the survey based on a table of random numbers or simply select every tenth task (or whatever interval you choose). In a stratified sample, you classify the tasks into groups of the most important, important, and less important and take a random sample from each group.

There is no accepted formula for determining the size of a sample. Keep it generally to no less than ten percent. Be wary of data collected on fewer than five people.

In constructing the follow-up survey, you follow the same rules for format as in the examples for block 30.1. There are two additions. Include directions and an envelope for return mail, and provide your telephone number for responding to questions. An administrative task includes keeping a roster of the recipients of the survey, logging the returns, and following up on nonrespondents.

Figure 32 is an abbreviated sample of a mailed survey form for trainees to complete. Simply by changing the directions at the top slightly and the pronouns in the statements and responses, you can use the same format for work group supervisors. Supervisor opinions are of utmost importance. In a sense, they are your end-user clients.

Mailed surveys are slow and sometimes not faithfully completed. If at all possible, go to the work locations, sit down with the people, and use the survey as an interview tool. The results are faster and more accurate (but don't intimidate), and you will pick up other ideas on how to improve training.

The other way to collect job application data, work observation, is less organized. You can assign an instructor to the

CURRICULUM FOLLOW-UP

Dear _____      _____
                          Name                                              Soc. Sec. No.

you completed _____ on _____
                          Program                           End Date

PURPOSE: As promised, here is a follow-up survey to help us improve the curriculum. Your candid and
prompt response will be used in curriculum revision.

DIRECTIONS: At the left is a listing of job tasks. At the right of each task is one disclaimer (I have not
performed this task.) and three rating statements (Training fully prepared me. Training partially prepared
me. Training did not prepare me.). Check the appropriate statement.

Return the survey promptly in the attached envelope. In case you have questions, my phone number is
(111) 333-5555.

1. Projected the life of a photoelectric cell.     ☐ I have not performed this task.
                                                   ☐ Training fully prepared me.
                                                   ☐ Training partially prepared me.
                                                   ☐ Training did not prepare me.

Please comment on how the training program could be improved:

_____

_____

_____

_____

END

Figure 32.  Sample mailed survey form (abbreviated) for trainees to
complete.

work site for periods of time to observe the work. You cannot
ensure that they will see the tasks you have selected. You
will need a more flexible measuring instrument. Figure 33
is an example.

Once the data from blocks 30.1 and 30.2 are collected and
integrated or determined to stand alone in block 30.3, reports
are issued. The reports, as noted earlier, include the assimilated data, your conclusions (what does it mean—positive,
neutral, or negative), and your recommendations (to change
or not to change). The reports are then distributed to the
curriculum committee, and a meeting date is set.

## Tips on Curriculum Committee Judgments

Committees are, no matter what the title, still committees.
Committees have a personality—a structure that tries to

```
┌─────────────────────────────────────────────────────────────────────┐
│                                                                       │
│                      WORK OBSERVATION REPORT                          │
│                                                                       │
│  ─────────────────────────────────────────      ──────────────────   │
│            Observer's Name                              Date          │
│                                                                       │
│  ─────────────────────────────────────────      ──────────────────   │
│       Person and Job Position Observed                 Date          │
│                                                                       │
│  1. Was the task performed safely? (Note discrepancies)               │
│                                                                       │
│                                                                       │
│  2. Was the task performed with the proper tools and equipment? (Note discrepancies) │
│                                                                       │
│                                                                       │
│  3. Was the task performed in a well-organized manner? (Note discrepancies) │
│                                                                       │
│                                                                       │
│  4. Was the task performed in a timely manner? (Note discrepancies)   │
│                                                                       │
│                                                                       │
│  5. Was the task completed properly?                                  │
│                                                                       │
│                                                                       │
│  Other comments:                                                      │
│                                                                       │
│                                                                       │
│                               END                                     │
│                                                                       │
└─────────────────────────────────────────────────────────────────────┘
```

Figure 33. Sample work observation report form.

emerge—regardless of the purpose or title of the committee. You can't stop the interplay of dominance and submission, loud and quiet, helpful and hurtful from occurring. You can, however, manage the situation. Here are some committee management tips:

- Establish the date, place, time, and purpose of the meeting as far in advance as possible.

- Send out the written material no earlier than one month and no less than two weeks in advance. Include an agenda.

- Call the week before to ensure the material was received, remind committee members of the meeting, and go over questions on the agenda.

- Prepare the meeting room the evening before (flip charts, seating arrangements, note pads, etc.).

- Have directions posted at entrances on how to reach the meeting room. Provide coffee, rolls, tea, soft drinks.

- Give members time to adjust their thinking to the current situation. Let them get their greetings, kidding, and immediate business out of the way.

- Start the meeting with introductions (if required).

- State the purpose of the meeting (Why are we here? To advise or dictate?).

- State the desired outcome of the meeting (recommendations on directions for change).

- Make clear whether decisions will be democratic (vote) or autocratic (made by one person).

- Work through the agenda, making sure each member speaks up and takes a stand.

- Take appropriate breaks.

- Form conclusions. Don't allow referral to other committees.

- Read back the major decision from the recorder.

- Adjourn with words of praise.

A curriculum committee has the power to change the curriculum based on their evaluation. They may want to jump to a solution. But their role is to recommend change. Your role, as the training professional, is to recommend the specific nature of the change. Judgment is the issue.

The purpose of evaluating curriculum is to decide whether the curriculum is all right or whether it should be changed. The decision should be based on hard data, but people must judge the data.

Perhaps you noticed that evaluation of instruction—how well the instructors taught—was not an element in the curriculum evaluation scheme presented in this chapter. As a member of training management, staff evaluation is your job, and you supervise it daily. A curriculum committee's business ends with curriculum. Assessing how well your staff carries out its duties, including instruction, is your responsibility; you must assess the quality of instruction.

# 11
# Evaluating Staff

More meaningless words have been written about staff evaluation than any other supervisory task. The more literature you read and workshops you attend, the less you know. It would be hard to find an area with more mixed messages and more pure nonsense.

Why is staff evaluation so difficult? Is it difficult, or do we just make it that way? There are at least three reasons why the evaluation water is muddy and confusion reigns. First, we are seeking the magic bullet, the secret, where none exists. Evaluation is hard work. It is hard work for the second reason: it's against our nature to tell others what we really think of them. It is more than uncomfortable, it is threatening. We buy the fad systems to get us out of the situation rather than being honest, which leads to the third reason: we don't know why being honest is worthwhile. We don't have a believable goal for staff evaluation. Evaluations don't seem to make much difference in the way the staff, as a whole, performs. We lack a philosophy of evaluation, which would help us establish the goal for a system. HRT demands honesty. Lives and megabucks depend on the quality of training, and the day-to-day quality of training depends on the honesty of your evaluations.

This chapter presents ways to evaluate the staff. You will need to analyze current staff evaluation practices, create a philosophy for staff evaluation, design an evaluation system, construct judgmental evaluation instruments, and communicate evaluation results.

## Analyzing Current Practices

There are five elements to investigate in existing staff evaluation programs:

- Purpose
- Methodology
- Instruments
- Feedback
- Impact

Let's work through two types of evaluation systems that most commonly exist in HRT functions: annual performance appraisal and in-classroom instructor evaluations. Annual performance appraisals offer many *purposes* to false organizational gods, for example, to increase productivity, provide feedback to staff, provide a basis for merit pay, improve performance, establish documentation for promotion, and provide an opportunity for career counseling. Can so many purposes be fulfilled through one appraisal that always begins with, "Well, there aren't any good evaluation systems, however. . . ."

Another problem is that the *methodology* is usually weak. Evaluation is typically a once-a-year affair (or change of job situation) that rarely requires, or has the system to collect, data throughout the year. A recent success or failure will color the evaluation. There is no way in most existing systems to average out the year.

Evaluation *instruments* are normally limited to one or two pages with an opportunity (or requirement) to add a personalized written paragraph or two. The concepts or practices to be "graded" are exceptionally general in nature and tend to be grouped under broad headings such as communication, leadership, fiscal control, and so forth. What do such broad terms mean? "Communicates clearly and concisely in all situations? Yes, No, Sometimes" is an example. Rarely could a person be marked yes. Marking no is just as rare (but makes sense based on the question). Yet, we know that to mark no may adversely and unfairly affect the person's career. So, the format forces you to mark sometimes—for virtually everyone. It does not help you discriminate the quality of a staff member's work. The instrument is a poor measuring device.

The *feedback* of the annual appraisal is weak because it only occurs annually. Time is spent in explaining and apologizing for the form. A once-a-year pat on the back (or kick in the rear) has a short motivation range.

What is the *impact* of the evaluation under most systems today? Assuming there is a clearly defined and achievable purpose, was it achieved? Did productivity improve? Were people given a true merit raise or promotion? Or, is it business as usual where the annual appraisal is only tangentially related to salaries, promotions, job assignments, and retention? The appraisal usually has no impact on proficiency and productivity. Consider: Annual appraisals today are most effective in building a paper trail to support dismissal; beyond that, they have little use.

As another example, in-class evaluation of instructors is the most common evaluation conducted in the training business. What might be the purpose of such evaluations?

The typical answer is to increase instructors' skills. A second answer is to ensure compliance with a procedure (e.g., administering examinations in the prescribed manner). The typical methodology and instrument rip the guts out of achieving the purpose. The supervisor slips quietly into the rear of the room and spends twenty minutes noisily flipping through the pages of the evaluation form. Twenty minutes! Using a homemade or adopted form! Feedback is usually a walk-down of the form with the supervisor (who may or may not have been an excellent instructor) offering some coaching. And, although the impact is higher because the evaluation is personalized and time is taken by management to visit the working environment, the quality of the impact can be no higher than the quality of the measuring instrument and observation ability of the supervisor.

You need a better evaluation system that will really work for you. The place to start is with a philosophy of evaluation.

## Philosophy of Evaluation

Without a valid philosophy of evaluation, the system will be purposeless. Let's start with the concept of philosophy, which is often misunderstood. The original root words, *philo* and *sophy*, meant love of knowledge. The use of it—even in the Golden Age of Greece, when Socrates, Plato, and Aristotle walked the barren hills of Athenia—meant well-rounded, knowledgeable, or, more aptly, having a holistic view of the world. Any educated person in that day was called a philosopher. There were no learned specializations like engineering, medicine, or law. People were educated in the "knowledge of the times." Philosophy meant to have a whole view.

That meaning still holds. The most successful people are those with a "whole view" of a business or an operation or an organization. They develop a philosophy because empirical data and advisors alone will not provide all the information they require to make correct decisions. Their whole view fills in the gaps between data and gives them a philosophy on which to base a judgment.

Developing a philosophy of evaluation begins with having a holistic view of the role of HRT. An analogy can be drawn from the world of retailing. Some discount stores you enter provide rows and rows of merchandise. You have to find everything yourself and sometimes help the clerk get the correct price and total the cost. Such stores represent one philosophy of retailing. Selling in large quantities is profitable and helps keep the price down.

If, however, you want clothing for a special event, you don't go to a discount outlet. The store you select will be specialized. From the moment you walk in the door, there's a different air, selected displays, and knowledgeable people to assist you. You know this difference is going to cost, but you also know you will get your money's worth. These stores have a different philosophy of retailing.

HRT is indeed specialized and expensive, and it requires its own philosophy. It caters to a unique market. From the moment people walk through the door, they must be struck by the air of a serious, no-nonsense, get-it-done environment for learning. It doesn't have to be as dull as an old college library. But the learning environment must be apparent.

A learning environment is created by the demands of both the technology and the ways people interact, which means not only the way the staff implements the technology, but also the way staff members interact with other staff members, trainees, work group supervisors, and others (board members, senior management, and other parts of the organization).

Therein lies the built-in problem with HRT. You select or assign staff members based on their technical expertise and your best estimate of how well they will learn the training business. They're in their second, third, or perhaps fourth career. They bring with them the behaviors they perceive as having been successful in past jobs. They believe themselves to be good at what they do. The problem is that HRT is a new technology, and the learning environment conducive to quality in learning is different from their past environments. They have to grow into the new technology and the new environment. How do you help? You begin the growing with a philosophy.

A statement of philosophy on anything has three parts: values, goals, and methods. The *value* statement tells what you believe. The *goal* statement tells where you are going. The *method* statement tells how you will reach the goal. Let's begin with an overall philosophy for HRT:

**HRT Philosophy:**

> *Value:*  HRT is a critical component in the safe and efficient operation of high-technology ventures.

> *Goal:*  HRT transmits the values, knowledges, and skills required for the safety and efficiency of workers.

> *Method:*  HRT staff utilizes the most current and proven effective training technologies and creates an environment that significantly contributes to the quality of learning.

That statement of philosophy becomes the hub of a wheel where each spoke is another philosophy, a subphilosophy, if you will. Curriculum, staff development, procedures, and so on, including staff evaluation, would all be spokes on this philosophical wheel. Let's look next at a philosophy for HRT staff evaluation:

**HRT Staff Evaluation Philosophy:**

*Value:* The most important contribution to the quality of training is the quality of the training staff.

*Goal:* The staff is continually assisted to create and improve learning technology and the learning environment.

*Method:* The staff is evaluated on the implementation and operation of the training technology and the state of the learning environment. The evaluations are conducted in a reliable and valid manner.

You now have a general framework from which to draw. Clearly, an annual appraisal and in-classroom snapshots are inadequate to support the goal. To help the staff know how well they are doing with the technology and environment requires a full-scope evaluation program.

## Designing Staff Evaluations

You have a philosophy of staff evaluation drawn from a philosophy of training. The statement recognizes, but does not specifically state, that HRT staff members come with diverse backgrounds and have to learn HRT technologies and environment. Implicit in the goal statement is that staff evaluation will occur at regular intervals (continually). In addition, the purpose of staff evaluation is to help (assist) the staff improve the quality of their work (as a means of improving the quality of training). The method statement makes clear the two areas of evaluation: (1) the implementation and operation of training technology and (2) the state of the learning environment.

We know why, who, what, and when. Now we have to establish how. There are a few knowns about evaluation to consider. Because there are not enough knowns to make up a science, these points are a bit jumpy. Yet, they will help in the design of the system:

- People change based on feedback. The amount of change does not appear to be directly tied to the source of the feedback. Instructors will change based on feedback from trainees, supervisors, peers, and self-evaluation via videotape. The source is not the force.

- People are more receptive to evaluations when they are new on the job. After some longevity, they need systems for conducting a personal evaluation as they step forward beyond the basic model of behavior the evaluation system established.

- Any evaluation scheme can be subverted and misused by any party involved. Checks and balances and redundancies are needed, but someone dedicated to subverting the system can do so, no matter how much money you pour into the backup system.

- Stringent evaluation systems can rob people of their creativity and the organization of the benefit of innovation.

- All evaluations of training staff are subjective. Even if empirical numbers are included (number of trainees who completed certification), the data must be judged in light of opportunity and meaning.

- Mixed messages in the feedback cycle can kill the credibility of evaluation. All personnel conducting evaluations need training on the forms, procedures, and techniques of feedback.

- The long-living adage that staff involvement in program development causes some type of an automatic endorsement may not be true in staff evaluation. The first problem is that a diverse staff may not know enough to have a meaningful input. Secondly, the staff may fully expect the leadership to provide the criteria for excellence.

With these disjointed points in mind, let's look at procedures for staff evaluation (the format is the one illustrated in the Appendix, minus the cover sheet):

1.0     Intent

     This procedure describes the steps in conducting evaluations of the training staff. It applies to incumbents in permanent positions.

2.0     Philosophy

     The most important contribution to the quality of the training is the quality of the training staff. The staff is continually creating and improving learning technology and the learning environment. The staff shall be evaluated on the implementation and operation of the training technology and the state of the learning environment. The evaluation shall be conducted in a reliable and valid manner.

3.0 References

3.1 Landy, Frank I., and James L. Farr. (1985). *The Measurement of Work Performance.* New York: Harcourt, Brace, Jovanovich Publishers.

3.2 Centra, John A. (1980). *Determining Faculty Effectiveness.* San Francisco: Jossey-Bass.

3.3 Seldin, Peter. (1980). *Successful Facility Evaluation Programs.* Crugers, NY: Coventry Press.

4.0 Definitions

4.1 Evaluation: The process of collecting empirical and subjective data and judging its worth.

4.2 Measuring instrument: Pencil-and-paper form with rating or ranking scales for selected concepts.

4.3 Self-evaluation: The process of judging one's self by the use of electronic recording devices and measuring instruments.

4.4 Peer evaluation: Judgments by co-workers using the evaluation system.

4.5 Supervisory evaluation: Judgments by supervisors using the evaluation system.

4.6 Trainee evaluation: Judgments by trainees using the evaluation system.

5.0    Responsibilities

    5.1    Manager–HRT

        5.1.1    Ensures all HRT personnel are trained to use the evaluation system.

        5.1.2    Approves all evaluation forms, changes, and revisions.

        5.1.3    Ensures all personnel are evaluated as scheduled.

        5.1.4    Meets annually with each staff member and reviews evaluation file.

        5.1.5    Issues annual report to senior decision makers on the impact of the evaluation system.

    5.2    Each HRT supervisor

        5.2.1    Conducts orientation of new staff members to the evaluation system.

        5.2.2    Conducts supervisory evaluation of staff members as required by schedule.

        5.2.3    Conducts peer evaluations of other supervisors as required by schedule.

        5.2.4    Assigns members of work group to conduct peer evaluations.

5.2.5   Reviews evaluation results with individual staff member within ten working days of the completion of each evaluation.

5.2.6   Forwards a quarterly report to Manager–HRT on the impact of evaluation.

5.3   Each HRT staff member

5.3.1   Conducts evaluations in a valid and reliable manner.

5.3.2   Implements evaluation recommendations.

5.3.3   Utilizes the professional grievance system when disagreeing with evaluation recommendations (HRT Professional Grievance HRTP–QC16.1).

6.0   Directions

6.1   To evaluate the implementation and maintenance of training technologies (Attachments 1 and 2) [figures 34 and 35]:

6.1.1   Per schedule, each staff member will be evaluated on the effectiveness of implementing training technologies.

6.1.2   Per schedule, each staff member will be evaluated on the efficiency in maintaining training technologies.

6.2 To evaluate the development and enhancement of a conducive learning environment (Attachments 1 and 2) [figures 34 and 35]:

6.2.1 Per schedule, each staff member will be evaluated on the quality and quantity of interaction with trainees, coworkers, training management, external personnel, and senior decision makers.

6.2.2 Per schedule, staff members will evaluate training manager on the quality and quantity of communications with staff members.

6.2.3 Per schedule, all staff members and manager will be evaluated on their achievements on increasing their professional and technical skills, knowledges, and abilities.

7.0 Records

After supervisory review, all completed evaluations are forwarded to Records for inclusion in each individual's confidential evaluation file. Access to each file is limited to the individual, supervisor of the individual, and the manager.

The procedure will have to be tailored for your organization, but it is a functional skeleton. The procedure clearly shows

**Attachment 1**

**STAFF EVALUATION SCHEDULE MATRIX**

|  | Management | Instructor | Support | Clerical |
|---|---|---|---|---|
| Organizational Performance Appraisal | A | A | A | A |
| Implementing Training Technology | Q | Q | Q | Q |
| Maintaining Training Technology | Q | Q | Q | Q |
| Interaction and Communication | Q | Q | Q | Q |
| Increasing Skills, Knowledges, and Abilities | Q | Q | Q | Q |

A = Annually
Q = Quarterly

Figure 34. Staff evaluation schedule matrix.

**Attachment 2**

**EVALUATION SOURCE MATRIX**

| TOPIC | Management | | | | Instructor | | | | Support | | | | Clerical | | | |
|---|---|---|---|---|---|---|---|---|---|---|---|---|---|---|---|---|
| Organizational Performance Appraisal | Sr Mgmt | | | | Sup | | | | Sup | | | | Sup | | | |
| Implementing Training Technology | Sr Mgmt | | | | Sup | | | | Sup | | | | Sup | | | |
| Maintaining Training Technology | Sr Mgmt | | | | Sup | | | | Sup | | | | Sup | | | |
| Interaction and Communication | 1Q Sup | 2Q Inst & Supp | 3Q Cler | 4Q Ext | 1Q Pr | 2Q Sup | 3Q Sf | 4Q Ext | 1Q Pr | 2Q Sup | 3Q Sf | 4Q Ext | 1Q Pr | 2Q Sup | 3Q Sf | 4Q Ext |
| Increasing Skills, Knowledges, and Abilities | 1Q Sup | 2Q Inst & Supp | 3Q Cler | 4Q Ext | 1Q Pr | 2Q Sup | 3Q Sf | 4Q Ext | 1Q Pr | 2Q Sup | 3Q Sf | 4Q Ext | 1Q Pr | 2Q Sup | 3Q Sf | 4Q Ext |

SOURCE

Cler = Clerical
Ext = External
Inst = Instructor
Pr = Peer
Sf = Self
Sr Mgmt = Senior decision makers
Sup = Supervisor
Supp = Support

Figure 35. Evaluation source matrix.

that evaluation is a two-way street. Everyone evaluates everyone else and self. In the evaluation source matrix (figure 35), an external evaluator is shown in the fourth quarter for the blocks on interaction and communication and on increasing skills, knowledges, and abilities. This approach is excellent. An outside look from other members of the organization, another training function, members of an advisory group, or professors from a local college can help. Make them use your forms. If they want to bring additional ones, that's fine, too. Forms—measuring instruments—are critical to the validity and continuity of the system.

### Constructing Judgmental Evaluation Forms

To strictly support the evaluation matrix would require the following instruments:

1. Organizational Performance Appraisal. Used for all HRT personnel.

2. Implementing Training Technology. Used for all HRT personnel.

3. Maintaining Training Technology. Used for all HRT personnel.

4. Interaction and Communication. Used for all HRT personnel.

5. Increasing Skills, Knowledges, and Abilities. Used for all staff with a series of attachments for each occupational specialization: managers and supervisors, instructors, each support specialty (curriculum, simulator fidelity, etc.), and clerical.

The same rules for developing instruments as described in chapter 10 apply in this situation: validity, reliability, directions, reverse questions, easy-to-use scales, and redundant questions on each construct, opinion, or behavior you decide to measure. And, the shorter the better. Be sure to leave space for written comments. Don't be afraid to measure the tough ones, like professionalism (you can define it in behavioral terms).

Let's go through each of the five categories and decide how to excel beyond current standards.

1. *Organizational performance appraisal.* You can always recommend changes in these usually ridiculous and poorly developed forms. Outside of that, you're stuck with the generality and lack of flexibility. The most productive activity is to organize the "written comments" section to fit HRT competencies. For example, have the supervisors categorize their comments under the headings you use in your continual evaluation system. The more numbers reflecting achievement, the better for reports going up the chain.

2. *Implementing training technology.* This instrument is an easy one to construct and complete but difficult to "pick the information from" for later computation and integration. Beyond the name, date, and other required headings, there's not much construction. The questions are: What new programs (or changes) are you implementing, and what evidence do you have that you are doing a good job? After you validate the evidence, you might help the computation and integration by rating the degree of success on the one-to-five scale. There is not much else to be done unless the MBO system (chapter 7) has built-in dates for stages of implementation (which it should have). In these cases, the evaluation processes become another project management tool (which it should be).

3. *Maintaining training technology.* The same can be said for this category that was said for the previous category. There are additional data points—audit findings, system failures, operation down time. There is not much beyond that data,

except recommendations made for systems or program improvements by the responsible party. Again, the evaluation becomes a forward-looking management tool. What were the recommendations? Why were or were not the recommendations acted upon?

4. *Interaction and communication.* Here is one you can get your creative teeth into. Interaction and communication can be verbal and nonverbal (the way someone frowns, crosses his or her arms, stares with a go-to-hell look, or smiles with arms open). Communication occurs in the classroom, simulator, hallways, over the phone, and in letters and memos. It may even be expressed by the way someone dresses.

You can look at the style and content of interaction and communication. Both can be judged with criteria that are anchored in performance and behaviors. The criteria also set the model, the example, the ideal. A statement of behavior or performance followed by a rating scale is okay, but there is a better way. The ambiguity can be reduced by using behavior-anchored rating scales (BARS) or performance-anchored rating scales (PARS). The difference in the title is subtle; you will do best to stay with performance as often as possible.

Figure 36 is an example of a PARS for written communication. The method of construction of the PARS on written communication was simple. Three constructs in written communication—mechanics, style, and content—were selected. Three statements for each construct at "less than," "equal to," and "more than" levels were written. Those are the only three statistical levels of existence. The use of dictionary and thesaurus helped come up with the appropriate words. Now, isn't the PARS on written communications better (because it draws a word picture) than the typical "Communicates clearly and concisely in all situations" with response options of yes, no, or sometimes?

**PARS FOR WRITTEN COMMUNICATION**

| Name of Person Being Evaluated | Job Position | Date | Period Covered (from-to) |

Directions: Work from right to left. First, read the performance statements in the column along the right. Then, read the descriptions of general performance level in the center column. Select which one of the three general performance levels is most accurate (refer back to the performance statements on the right if necessary). Finally, select one number from the numerical scale on the left. The scale rates the overall level of performance, with 9 corresponding to the highest level and 1 corresponding to the lowest level. Mark ( ) the number you selected, and write it in the space provided in the lower left-hand corner.

| NUMERICAL SCALE | GENERAL PERFORMANCE LEVEL | PERFORMANCE STATEMENTS |
| --- | --- | --- |
| 9<br><br>8<br><br>7 | Above-average clarity. Message travels well. Little effort is required by reader. | • Purpose of communication is clear, concise, and obtains results.<br>• The style is matched to the reader's background.<br>• Uses paragraph and sentence structure and punctuation to enhance the message. Word selection enhances message. |
| 6<br><br>5<br><br>4 | Average clarity. Message is understandable with some interpretation required by reader. | • Purpose of communication is usually clear and accurate and generally to the point.<br>• The style is direct and simple.<br>• Generally is correct in paragraph and sentence structure; word selection shows effort; adequate punctuation. |
| 3<br><br>2<br><br>1 | Lower-than-average clarity. Message is garbled, confusing. | • Purpose of communication is unclear; rambling, hazy, unfocused, obscure.<br>• The style is verbose and garrulous or constrained and limited.<br>• Lack of attention to paragraph and sentence structure, poor word selection, incorrect punctuation. |

Specific instances of performance and comments:

_____ numerical description for this factor.

Figure 36. Performance-anchored rating scale (PARS) for written communication.

Try it. Develop a PARS on oral communication. What might be three important constructs? Speech has two parts, the mechanical aspects of making the sound and the articulation of thoughts. The thoughts are less than, equal to, or above average in quality. The same comparisons can be completed with the sound of the voice. Another important PARS under this section is professional decorum. Work on it, clarify your expectations to the staff. Build a professional environment.

5. *Increasing skills, knowledges, and abilities.* This area is the easiest in which to develop PARS but because of breadth of job specialization requires the most time. The number of PARS that could be developed is unlimited. Just in the area of improving classroom skills are clarity of presentation, effectiveness of presentation, maintenance of trainees' interest, oral questioning techniques, lab safety, managing examinations, administration, and so forth. You can't just call the local public school and borrow the "check the blank" form used to evaluate teachers once a year. Those forms are not good enough for HRT!

---

**PARS FOR PROFESSIONAL INTEREST AND TECHNICAL GROWTH**

| Name of Person Being Evaluated | Job Position | Date | Period Covered (from-to) |

**Directions:** Work from right to left. First, read the performance statements in the column along the right. Then, read the descriptions of general performance level in the center column. Select which one of the three general performance levels is most accurate (refer back to the performance statements on the right if necessary). Finally, select one number from the numerical scale on the left. The scale rates the overall level of performance, with 9 corresponding to the highest level and 1 corresponding to the lowest level. Mark (  ) the number you selected, and write it in the space provided in the lower left-hand corner.

| NUMERICAL SCALE | GENERAL PERFORMANCE LEVEL | PERFORMANCE STATEMENTS |
|---|---|---|
| 9<br><br>8<br><br>7 | More than usual amount of typical activity or effort related to professional interest and technical growth. | • Seeks information about all technical areas.<br>• Seeks improvement in relevant technical developments.<br>• Works extra hours on own initiative to learn about new developments. |
| 6<br><br>5<br><br>4 | Usual amount of typical activity or effort related to professional interest and technical growth. | • Occasionally reads journals in related technical areas.<br>• Interest in new technology is usually limited to own area only.<br>• Sometimes displays a negative attitude toward new ideas. |
| 3<br><br>2<br><br>1 | Less than usual amount of typical activity or effort related to professional interest and technical growth. | • Is pessimistic and cynical about new technical developments.<br>• Has little curiosity about technologies related to own specific area.<br>• Adopts an attitude of "if it's important, someone will tell me about it" toward developments. |

Specific instances of this individual's work activities related to this factor:

_____ numerical description for this factor.

Figure 37. Performance-anchored rating scale (PARS) for professional interest and technical growth.

Review the following PARS, figure 37, on keeping up-to-date. This one concentrates on a single issue (of many possible in that area): professional interest and technical growth. It could work for all staff members regardless of job.

PARS are not ways to achieve mind control. PARS must not be used to implement values alien to staff members' ideals. Stay away from such constructs as self-esteem, personality characteristics, or anything that smacks of faddish cultism. PARS are a businesslike way to add substance to evaluation judgments. Once your evaluation system is in place, there is the need to communicate the results. There are two populations and two results.

## Communicating Evaluation Results

There are two groups to whom the results of evaluation must be communicated: each person evaluated, in an individual and private meeting, and the entire staff (including senior management), in a grouped data mode.

The various individual evaluations occur in a quarterly fashion. The purpose of the frequency is to keep the staff and management of HRT focused on growth, development, and improvement. To maintain the vitality of evaluation as a vehicle for positive change requires enthusiasm for all individual meetings. Each meeting is formally scheduled and judiciously attended without failure. The meetings are serious, businesslike (all paperwork is on the desk in a neat file), and positively oriented. Do not allow the meetings to become casual or frequently postponed. Your supervision is required to ensure that the evaluation environment is kept professional.

The second communication process, the group data on evaluation, must be made into an annual event. The procedure requires an annual report. Make the publication slick. Use it to show the truth. Don't let "evaluation creep" (gradual rising of ranking because of familiarity) occur. Enforce strict standards, compile the data into reports using the actual evaluation forms, and show this year's measure as compared to the past.

This annual report approach allows two side-payments. First, it demonstrates the positive impact of an effective evaluation system, return on investment of money. Second, it provides an opportunity to evaluate the evaluation component. Perhaps your entire system is composed of fifty PARS. Some may need improvement; others may need to be scrapped and new ones developed. Each year, seize the opportunity to evaluate your evaluation system. There are several ways to accomplish such an evaluation. An effective way is to compare the impact of the evaluations to the goal(s) established in your evaluation philosophy.

An HRT function requires—demands—that everything be superior. Evaluation of the staff, as colleagues, is the way to achieve true competency in teaching others how to survive in dangerous environments.

# 12
# Evaluating Procedures

Procedures are a communication system. The major thrust of the system is to provide control by giving directions and mandating reports. As a communication system, they can be evaluated in a direct manner.

This chapter presents ways to evaluate procedures. You will need to know the evaluation points in the communication cycle, how to develop measuring instruments for each point, how to use existing sources of evaluation data, and methods of introducing change to the system.

## Effectiveness and Efficiency

Evaluating procedures requires an investigation of the efficiency of each procedure and the effectiveness of the procedure system. The evaluation of efficiency and effectiveness can be accomplished at the same time by again using the communication cycle given in figure 9 in chapter 4. The communication cycle can also be used for evaluating written communication.

Given the communication cycle and the procedure system, see whether you agree with the logic of the following evaluation points:

- Writing ability of sender.

- Critiquing ability of reviewers.

- Distortion of communication—"noise"—caused by reliance solely on the written word and line drawings.

- Adequacy of the distribution system, which affects availability of the procedures to the receivers.

- Capability and inclination of the receiver to follow the procedure.

- Existence and endurance of the "close-the-loop" report giving feedback to prove the task was accomplished in compliance with the procedure.

An effective direction-giving system is one where directions are given and work is accomplished with feedback providing proof. The evaluation of the effectiveness of the system becomes a matter of checking records for the end-of-cycle reports and monitoring productivity.

But you also need to know how efficiently the system works. How well the system works depends on the human factors of the situation. Human factors are easy to deal with when you are considering the interface between a person and a machine. For example, Knob A and Knob B must be turned at the same time to start System X. Knob A is five feet away from Knob B. Can the operator see the exact setting when stretched so far? The machine may be marvelous on paper, but if it is clumsy to operate, it loses efficiency. Let's transfer that type of problem to written procedures. The procedure-communication cycle—from originator's message to receiver's task accomplishment and feedback—may entail a requirement that is just as clumsy. The review cycle may be overdone, or the directions in the procedure may require too much coordination, too many "knobs" to turn at the same time.

With these thoughts in mind, let's consider how to develop some measuring instruments.

## Measuring Instruments Development

The construction of a measuring instrument for procedures would appear to require three sections: efficiency in the development and distribution of procedures, efficiency in the use of the procedures, and effectiveness of the procedures. Consider the sample documents given in figures 38, 39, and 40. You perhaps noticed there were no reversed questions in figure 38. The redundancy check is accomplished by the interview with the supervisor and by repeating some of the questions in the survey of the end-users (figure 39).

The best way to complete the end-user form, figure 39, is by interview. A mailing may include many who have not yet used the procedure. A telephone call is quick and easy. Face-to-face is even better when logistics allow.

The third evaluation form, figure 40, is the effectiveness check. It is conducted in the records system and has one problem. Although "close-the-loop" forms will demonstrate the work was accomplished, there is no way to know how many attempts were aborted. There is no odometer on procedures, no way to tell how many times the pages were turned. There are at least two strategies you can invoke. One is going to records and sampling the close-the-loop documents for all procedures and auditing them for discrepancies in the completion of forms. That approach will provide a small

---

**EVALUATION OF PROCEDURE DEVELOPMENT AND DISTRIBUTION**

Directions: This form is to be completed by each originator of a new procedure and by each originator of a major procedure revision. The statements on the left are followed by Yes–No blocks on the right. Check the appropriate block. Space is provided under each statement for comments about improving the system. After you complete the form, meet with your supervisor who will review your responses. This form will then be signed by the supervisor, who will forward it to Records.

1. Before developing the procedure, I clearly understood the purpose of
   the procedure ...............................................   ☐ Yes   ☐ No

2. The end-users of the procedure were identified ....................   ☐ Yes   ☐ No

3. I was aware of the capacity of the end-users to understand the
   terminology and wrote the procedure with their level of understanding
   in mind ......................................................   ☐ Yes   ☐ No

4. There was adequate clerical support during the writing and rewriting
   stages .......................................................   ☐ Yes   ☐ No

5. The reviewers were timely and increased the quality of the
   procedures ...................................................   ☐ Yes   ☐ No

6. I have followed up with the end-users to make sure the procedure is
   available and usable .........................................   ☐ Yes   ☐ No

7. The procedure on procedures was an excellent guide throughout the
   process.......................................................   ☐ Yes   ☐ No

---

Title of Procedure                          Number          Effective Date

_____ / _____   _____   _____
Print Name            Signature             Job Position      Date Form
of Originator                                                 Completed

_____ / _____   _____   _____
Print Name            Signature             Job Position      Date of Interview
of Reviewing Supervisor

END

Figure 38.  Sample form for evaluating procedure development and
distribution.

amount of information about the system and the form, but it will probably identify more people problems than system problems (which, although needed, is not your purpose in procedure evaluation).

The other strategy is a longitudinal approach to measure effectiveness of the procedures. Select a category of procedures, say curriculum, to track for a specific time frame, for example, a month or a quarter. Dig into the MBR system (chapter 7), and identify how much procedurally controlled curriculum work is to be done during that period. For demonstration, suppose you identify fifty revisions. At the end

---

**EVALUATION OF PROCEDURE USEFULNESS TO THE END-USER**

Directions:

Procedure _____
                            Title                                  Number

was recently published or reissued. Please take a few minutes of your time to help us judge the quality of the procedure. The statements on the left are followed by Yes–No blocks. Check the appropriate blocks. Space is provided under each phrase for comments. Please return this form to HRT in the attached envelope. Thank you.

1. The procedure was needed ........................................ □ Yes   □ No

2. The procedure is easily available to me ........................... □ Yes   □ No

3. The procedure is easy to understand ............................. □ Yes   □ No

4. The instruction steps are well thought out and match the work flow ... □ Yes   □ No

5. The forms are simple to complete ............................... □ Yes   □ No

6. It's clear where the completed forms are to be sent ................ □ Yes   □ No

7. Overall it's a quality procedure ................................... □ Yes   □ No

_____ / _____    _____    _____
**Print Name**               **Signature**             **Job Position**       **Date Form**
**of Originator**                                                   **Completed**

_____ / _____    _____    _____
**Print Name**               **Signature**              **Job Position**       **Date of Interview**
**of Reviewing Supervisor**

**Is follow-up action required?**    □ Yes   □ No

**END**

---

Figure 39. Sample form for evaluating the usefulness of a procedure.

of the time frame, go to records and audit the close-the-loop forms. You are looking for what's not there, not completed. Work your way back through the chain and find out why. People? Resources? Or, the procedure system has too many loops in it?

About the only way to format such an evaluation and have a final report is to utilize an annotated report approach, figure 40. It can be as official a document as any other, but it has a severe limitation in that it lacks a methodology for assimilation with other data. Figure 40 is a completed example of the form.

---

**ANNOTATED EVALUATION OF PROCEDURE SYSTEM EFFECTIVENESS**

Directions: Fill in the blanks in the first section. The remainder of the form, with attachments as needed, is used for listing discrepancies and recommended actions for correction. After you complete the form, meet with the Manager–HRT, who will review the evaluation. This form will be signed by the manager, who will forward it to Records. Write the word END on the last page of the attachments you include.

1. The category of procedures selected for an effectiveness evaluation was ____curriculum____.
List each title and number.

2. The time frame selected for evaluation was _1 June 19xx to 1 October 19xx._.

3. The number of forms estimated for transactions during the time frame was __50__.
The number estimate was based on (explain): _research_.

4. The number of forms actually transacted was __39__.

5. Other forms not estimated but transacted during the time frame were _____.

6. Of the difference between the numbers in questions 3 and 4 (write in difference) __11__, what were the reasons?

7. List each discrepancy and recommended action to be taken.

   7.1 Discrepancy: _The forms were not submitted because the curriculum changes were not accomplished. Workload was the reason given_.
   Recommendation: _Meet with supervisor of area_.

   7.2 Discrepancy: _Four forms were hung up in the sign-off system. Vacation was the reason given_.
   Recommendation: _Develop an alternative sign-off authority_.

   7.3 Discrepancy: _Four forms were unaccounted for, apparently lost in the system. That is 8 percent of the initial number being traced_.
   Recommendation: _Immediate personal interview with all involved_.

 

 

HRT Manager's Signature                            Date

END

---

Figure 40. Sample completed form of an annotated evaluation report on the effectiveness of the procedure system.

The annotated approach is like fishing in the ocean. You never know what you will catch. The missing 8 percent (one of the discrepancies in figure 40), if generalized to the entire system, is an exceptionally significant deficiency and demands immediate corrective action. Additional sources of existing data—data that have already been collected—can assist you in determining the source of the problem.

## Existing Sources of Evaluation Data

HRT functions are continually assisted in their evaluation efforts by internal and external audits and inspections. Because the results of such investigations are brought to the attention of senior decision makers, there is an effort to solve the specific problems as rapidly as possible. (Get it solved, and get it out of the way.) The rush to get out of trouble sometimes washes away a consideration of the root cause of a problem. Audits are samples of what is or is not going on; they are not designed to cover everything. View audit findings as symptoms, not as an identification of the illness.

Take some time. Construct a matrix, with findings across the top and possible reasons down the side. Think, Do we have a people problem, system problem, audit problem, communication problem, other problem, or a combination? Research the situation. Get some true benefit out of audits.

Another simple index can be used to evaluate potential problems with the procedure system: staff grumbling and requests for exceptions. Grumbling is a bit difficult to track, but listen. One sign of a problem is when most of the people using a specific procedure request an exception. You can also learn of a problem by talking to clerks about the completion and filing (in Records) of the forms. If you discover significant problems and decide to change the system, there are some change strategies to consider.

## Methods of Introducing Change

There are three additional choices for introducing change in a closed-loop procedure system:

- Trash the entire system at midnight on the 31st, and put the new one in place.

- Change one component (e.g., the new review cycle), and see if it works without disrupting the rest of the system.

- Make piecemeal changes in a random fashion (which violates the concept of a closed system).

There is another less conventional but exceptionally effective way:

- Select one subgroup of the HRT function (for example, the evaluation group). Implement the new procedure system in the one subgroup. Study, study, study. It is not a bad way to check out any kind of major change.

The evaluation of a procedure system is difficult because the system is moving and there are many confounding factors. Yet, the system is a communication system, a way of giving directions, and it must be respected for its power—the power to control work processes. Your most astute efforts will be required to make it work correctly. Your diligence in evaluating the efficiency and effectiveness of the system will result in continual improvement—a fine-tuning, if you will—of the procedures that make HRT work.

# 13
# Evaluating Records

The records function is the center for documentation. There information comes in and is integrated, packaged, and sent out to users. This chapter presents ways to evaluate the records function. There is no mystique about it. You must know how to check the validity of the incoming information, measure the capability of the records systems to integrate and package data, and judge the acceptability of the timeliness of reports.

## Validity of Incoming Information

Two points must be checked for input validity: the accuracy when it arrives at the input clerks' terminals and the accuracy of the actual input. Whether the system is a manual pencil-and-paper one, a data clerk keyboarding into a computer, or an optical-scan input system doesn't matter. Accuracy is the issue, beginning with the input form.

Forms can be inaccurate because of human error and sloppiness, because they are confusing to complete, or because they are mutilated (the mail sorting machine ate it). One simple problem-logging sheet used by the input clerks will establish a tracking system. Figure 41 is an abbreviated

| | | | | | |
|---|---|---|---|---|---|
| **EVALUATION OF DATA RECEIVED** | | | | | |

Directions: Use this sheet when incoming forms are not accurate. Place the date received and form number on the left. Check the reason(s) to the right.

| | | PROBLEM(S) | | | |
|---|---|---|---|---|---|
| **DATE** | **FORM NUMBER** | **Readability** | **Error** | **Mutilation** | **Other (Specify)** |
| | | | | | |
| | | | | | |
| | | | | | |
| | | | | | |
| | | | | | |

Figure 41. Sample form for recording forms inaccurately completed.

example. It is not sophisticated. It doesn't need to be any more than a tracking system of rejected inputs. You must analyze the rejected input forms and determine whether you have a people problem or a form problem. Then take corrective action.

The second validity check is a verifying activity. Quite simply, it is a process of double-checking recently input data. The verifier may be the supervisor who randomly samples, or a clerk working on a rotating basis checking other clerks' work. Remedies usually hinge on resolving people problems or improving input procedure availability and use, or a combination.

Once the data are in the system, the problem is a bit different.

## System Capability to Integrate and Package Data

An excellent way to evaluate the ability of a system to integrate data is to feed in a test load that contains all data elements.

Work out the integration by another means (hand, calculator, another computer), and compare the two sets of results. Perform the test under varying system conditions (e.g., heavy load, light load). What's lost? What's gained?

If there are some problems, the fixes lay in the software or the hardware capabilities. There aren't many management alternatives; change software or add power to the hardware. Data come out in straight-line printing, tables, and graphics. If you think the configuration of the output could be improved, you need a software solution. There are two software choices: off-the-shelf or custom. Off-the-shelf software never gives you exactly what you want, but it is less costly than custom programs. Before investing in additional software, have the proposed configurations evaluated by other end-users. It takes time to correct a system. You don't want to pay for poor improvements; make sure you take the time to identify the right changes to be made.

## Timeliness of Reports

Training reports are used in a variety of ways. Work group supervisors will use the data on training completed and training needed as a critical planning tool for scheduling. Trainees will utilize their individual reports in their career planning. Senior decision makers will evaluate a work group's readiness to perform efficiently based on the amount of training coupled with end-of-course scores. Training management will look at all the reports for a wide assortment of purposes such as planning, setting class schedules, assigning work, tracking accomplishments, building budgets, and performing evaluations. Instructors will use reports for counseling trainees.

People will come to depend on the reports. When the reports do not come out on time, they will begin to lose confidence in the system. Random checking, by yourself, with the users is well worth your time. Phone calls are good; you may also discover that there are problems with the internal mail distribution system. On the other hand, if you discover that the reports are not being generated on schedule, you are back to the issue of having a people problem or a system problem. With a system problem, be sure to investigate the reality of your reports schedule in light of the computer load. Often computers sit idle, and then everyone wants to use them at once. Some commitments to off-peak use can contribute to timeliness.

Evaluating records is absolute simplicity. The data are valid or invalid. The system integrates or does not. The reports are timely or not. The fixes are supervision, management, and allocation of resources.

HRT has sophisticated needs. Every possible technology that can contribute must be utilized in delivering effective training. Part 4, Training through Simulation, presents proven ways to achieve increased learning through the use of simulation and simulators. The potential for effective learning is geometrically greater than traditional approaches.

# Part 4: Training through Simulation

Training with part-task, full-scope, and field simulation is here, today! It is no longer science fiction. *Simulation training* is used by medical schools, police academies, nuclear power plants, commercial airlines, and every branch of the United States military. The cost of a simulator runs from a few thousand dollars to more than $20 million. Used ineffectively, a $20-million simulator is not only a waste, it is dangerous. No discussion of high-risk training would be complete without describing how to use simulation training to cause effective learning.

Chapter 14, Simulation Management, takes you through the potential of simulation, terminology, fidelity management, and how to reap some side-payments from the simulator. Chapter 15, Simulation Scenario Development, shows how to develop ways to match trainees with the learning levels and goals of scenarios to achieve maximum learning. The misuse of scenarios is covered, and ways to develop scenarios are demonstrated. A format for scenarios is prescribed along with ways to control the actual written content of the scenario. Chapter 16, Simulation Instruction Methods, closes out the section with a field-proven way to cause better simulation instruction. It centers on the question-mapping technique and provides all the forms and methods needed to set up your own instructor training program.

# 14
# Simulation Management

The ultimate purpose of placing trainees into a simulated working environment is to evaluate their judgments. That end purpose is the same regardless of the field of work—law, health and medicine, flight, defense, finance, or whatever. True simulation instruction moves you past panels, consoles, pictures, and mock-ups into the world beyond facts where trainees must exercise judgment.

Judgments to solve a problem must be rendered by the trainees inside a specific time frame. That time frame includes the time for the physical manipulations and communications necessary to solve the problem. In simulation, problems can only be solved with the limited options available in the environment. These environments can, in real life, cause death, place the public at risk, or cause financial ruin. Judgment is what counts in these environments.

Judgment is the highest level of human thinking. Your brain stores up to 100 trillion bits of information. Your thoughts race through one trillion nerve cells at perhaps the speed of light. The simulated environment must force the issue, Can the trainee assimilate and render a technically correct judgment and properly implement the solution by manipulations and communication inside the time frame required to stave off disaster? To use the simulated environment for a lesser end purpose is not only a waste of resources but also shows absolute disregard for human life and the HRT profession.

You cannot teach trainees how to make judgments in an ever-changing environment where someone keeps moving first base. You can teach decision making, force technical information into the brain, and drill on procedures. Judgments are a higher level of thinking than factual decision making. The decisions that you teach are based on facts (e.g., the pressure goes down, therefore the immediate actions are....). Judgment is what is needed after the facts are washed away by circumstances. Judgment can't be taught, only scientifically evaluated.

This chapter presents ways to ensure that simulated environments are managed toward the end purpose of evaluating trainees' judgments. You will need to understand the core terminology of simulation, the types and levels of learning that can occur in a simulated environment, fidelity management, and additional uses of simulation.

## Simulation Technology

Beware of the mystique makers in simulation who intimidate by verbiage and are arrogant by nature. Using jargon words—like multivalue parameters, unacceptable algorithm, run-length control, hierarchical modeling, and thought-simulator testbed—only adds confusion to your world.

There is nothing new about simulation. Mankind has been around for a few million years. Only for about the last ten thousand have we been civilized. How do you suppose mankind lasted that long? Taking the young hunters out and throwing them against wild animals, or simulation? Thus, learning through simulation became the basis for cultural events, rites of passage, that are still celebrated today.

In World War I, wooden barrels were cut down and made into a seat. The cutout staves were used as rudder pedals and a stick. To obtain a feeling of movement, ropes would be pulled. Ed Link took it a step further and didn't use big words. In 1929, he slipped into the basement of his father's organ factory and rigged a cockpit mounted on a pneumatic organ bellow. He called it the "pilot-maker."

Simulation has always been used for training. Computerization is a new twist. Don't let it overwhelm you. Your goal is quality HRT, and there are only a few concepts and definitions you must understand to start toward achieving your goal of evaluating trainees' judgments.

- Full-scope computer-driven simulation: A simulator incorporating detailed modeling of the major systems, consoles, and panels of the referenced craft, plant, weapon, or situation.

- Part-task computer-driven simulation: A simulator incorporating detailed modeling of a limited number of the systems, consoles, and panels of the referenced craft, plant, or weapon or a limited number of real-life situations.

- Field simulation: Use of the natural environment to stage valid scenarios.

- Fidelity: Measurement of the degree the simulated environment replicates and reflects the workings of the real-life environment and situation.

- Real time: The simulated events unfold in the same time length as the true events.

- Malfunction: An apparent failure of simulated equipment or degradation of a situation that is programmed to occur for training purposes.

- Passive malfunction: Programmable failures of simulated equipment or degradation of a situation that does not become immediately evident.

- Freeze: A condition of placing the simulator or simulated environment in a static mode.

- Backtrack: Restoration of the simulator or simulated environment to a previous set of conditions.

- Snapshot: Storage of existing conditions at any selected point in time.

This basic core of terminology will get you started on the training side of the simulation business. Recalling the training concepts of development, utilization, and evaluation, let's examine what kind of learning can be achieved with simulation.

## Learning Potential in a Simulated Environment

Before entering a simulated environment, the trainee goes through a building progression of traditional training: lectures that present the theories, laboratory and shop courses that allow hands-on learning of nomenclature and the functioning of hardware, lecture and discussion classes on case studies of a problem-solving nature, and perhaps OJT or field tours.

The trainee now has the learning parts catalogued into separate nerve cells of the brain. The facts are there and have been tested. The theories and concepts are there and have been tested. The operating principles are there and have been tested. Hands-on application on pieces of the learning are there and have been tested. How do you tie it together? How is it possible for all the different pieces to become a functioning system of behavior? Look at how complex speech is: the Brocca area of the brain must create the correct words for accurate communication, the vocal cords must turn the words (thoughts) into sounds, and the motor strip in the frontal lobe of the brain must program muscular movements for speech. The behaviors that are desired as an outcome of HRT are often even more complex.

Let's take a quick tour of the three-pound, three-pint, greyish-yellow matter that we call the brain. The purpose of the tour is to better grasp the role of simulation in HRT. Information learned during the traditional training enters through the five senses of smell, touch, taste, sight, and hearing. The hippocampus, an S-shaped structure deep within both sides of the brain, has the job of sorting and organizing the information. To do that job, it uses one of two types of nerve cells, neurons. There are perhaps 100 billion neurons— more than there are stars in our galaxy. Picture neurons as surrealistic paintings of trees in the winter. Their branches are made of protein, draped with a gooey membrane, and studded with an enzyme called calpain.

When information comes into the hippocampus as an electrical impulse and is routed to the correct subcompartment of the brain, the throbs of the impulse cause the calpain to eat away or melt some of the branches of the neuron. That allows the gooey membrane to flow. The gooey stuff is called a neurotransmitter. The brain employs more than six dozen different types of these chemical messengers. The neurotransmitter flows over the narrow crevices between neurons, called synapses, and makes contact with other neurons. The linking is called a memory trace, and it has a duration.

Short-term memory allows you to punch a telephone number you just found in the directory and forget it at the first hello, or recall it for a few hours if you paid strict attention. Its average capacity is from five to nine bits (Ma Bell learned that decades ago).

Long-term memory is the goal. Here, if you will, the first fragile memory traces are strengthened and then preserved—bronzed like a pair of baby shoes. The long-term memory stays forever, although you may forget how to find it in your brain. The hippocampus, which also controls emotions, does a better job of bronzing for long-term memory if some feelings are involved with the memory. Three points about the bronzing of memory traces:

1. The better organized the information (instructional material) coming in, the higher the potential of it being bronzed in the right memory trace.

2. Memory traces are like trails in a forest; the more often they are traveled, the easier they are to find.

3. When the memory trace is wrong, or the world has changed (to eject you now pull this lever instead of flipping that switch), the bronzing has to be melted and reformed.

Now some points specific to simulation learning. The facts presented in lectures are stored in several different compartments of the thick folded outer covering of the brain called the cortex. The theories, concepts, and other higher-level thoughts are retained in the cerebellum, the cauliflower-shaped part in the lower back of the brain. Motor movements are directed by the front lobe of the brain. Simulation builds the ability of the brain to cross-reference—to search for, find, assimilate, and act on information stored in different parts of the brain—while correcting misbronzed memory traces. The traces are then strengthened by experience, via repetition, and become easier to find.

Simulation is a way to get the information organized, pull information together. It also shows the trainees where they have misbronzed information. Melting down the bronze is hard work; telling doesn't do it effectively. Doing—allowing the person to find out what is correct—is the effective learning method.

Simulation management takes into account how to organize simulated experiences to achieve the best long-term learning for different types and levels of learning. Let's examine each of eight kinds of learning, from orientation to judgment, to see how simulation enhances learning.

*Orientation.* A tour of a simulator or of an environment where activities will be simulated is an excellent motivation for trainees entering a new program. They obtain an idea of what they are up against. In-depth presentations are not needed. Use the presentation given to visiting big shots and add in how and when the simulator or field simulation fits into their program.

*Theory application.* Teaching and learning abstract concepts in a lecture is difficult. Showing helps get the information into the correct memory trace. The use of a systems simulator to show the relation of heat to pressure, drag to speed, vibration to stability, rate to pressure, and so forth, imprints the concept more effectively. Using more than one sense for input causes more neuron action. Just don't overload the circuits by introducing too much too soon.

*Single-system operation.* During classes on the operation of single systems, you can use simulation to tie hearing, seeing, and touch together for even more effective retention. Get the brain used to putting things together for action.

*Systems integration operation.* When several systems must be integrated, no longer can everything be articulated in the classroom. Simulation is there to pull all the neurons together, and simulation is a must at this point. In the medical field, there are eleven systems in the human body. A nuclear plant may have eighty systems. A military field simulation includes transportation, logistics, communications, fire power, and casualty management. Aircraft, space vehicles, and law enforcement vary in their number of systems, but the interaction of the systems gives you more than the sum of the parts. Learning by simulation is the most effective way to move memory traces out of classroom theory and into the learning of reality. One system is started, then another, and another, until all are functioning.

*Normal operation.* Once all systems are working, the trainee is in the full learning mode. There may well be a function of the brain that manages work processes, something like a built-in supervisor that causes the different memory traces to reorganize to accomplish different work tasks with the same information. The reordering is accomplished by drilling on different tasks, forcing the brain to be nimble, flexible, but learning a routine.

A point about instruction needs to be made. Sometimes simulator instructors, because of time or lack of understanding, fail to teach normal operations in simulation. They push forward and concentrate on problems. That approach is wrong. The brain needs a base of normality from which the senses can recognize off-normal situations and alert the brain to get busy and find the problem. You've had the experience, "Something doesn't feel right; I don't know what it is, but something is not right!" Your senses picked up on a change in normality. The red flag is raised, and the search is underway. That base of normality must be embedded in the brain. Afterwards, you move to the off-normal and diagnostics.

*Off-normal operation.* Begin with a minor malfunction in one system, work up to system failure, then move to systems failure. Once the diagnostics of immediate malfunctions are learned, go back to one system, and add a passive malfunction. Work all the way up to systems failure again.

Think about how memory traces are bronzed. Don't melt and rebuild the bronze more than needed. Long-term confusion can result. Always teach from simple to complex. Knowing a single emergency immediate-action drill is one thing. Diagnosing the problem and selecting the correct immediate-action drill from among many is another. Don't let the simulation activity be a confusion maker.

*Retraining and continuing training.* Retraining and continuing training are designed to keep the incumbents on their toes (retraining) and up-to-date with technology changes (continuing training). In retraining, your concentration must be on keeping the memory traces (the trails) easy to find in the brain. You don't do retraining on what the incumbents do daily. Concentrate on what they might have to do, things they don't get to experience frequently. Keep those trails well traveled.

Continuing training is a totally different ball game. Here you have to do some rebronzing. A couple of examples. Take out a blank piece of lined paper like you used in school and write your name on it. Go ahead, do it. Then write down the name of a flower, a color, and a number between one and seven.

Americans will typically write their names neatly in the upper right-hand corner. Then, they usually go to the left side of the page and write rose, red, and select the number three. (Different cultures will come up with different responses but will be consistent inside their culture.) The behavior is called a trained incapacity.

Another example: Has the following ever happened to you? You arise in the morning and rather automatically get ready for work. Some thought to your clothes, but generally you simply focus on getting out and getting to work. You go to your new car, slide in, enjoy the smell, and immediately try to put the key where the ignition was on your old car.

Such tricks of the mind are true trained incapacities because the memory traces are so strong that the responses are automatic. You don't want automatic behavior in the operating room, in the cockpit, or in the field when procedures have changed but habit carries over to action. Thus, one purpose of continuing training in simulation is drill on new technology.

A side issue, although not named, occurs frequently. The built-in supervisor in the brain doesn't like to be interrupted when resting. It's resting when the memory traces are working on automatic. The traces are so strong that no supervision is required. Have you ever been punching in a familiar phone number, had an interruption, and have (1) totally forgotten the rest of the number and had trouble recalling it or (2) forgotten where you were in the sequence? The supervisor in the mind was resting.

What's the consequence of such a situation to a reactor operator on a nuclear submarine? A law enforcement officer during an arrest? Point made? Continuing training has to focus on reordering the way the brain does business that the brain has dismissed as routine.

*Judgment.* Simulation training has the highest potential for evaluating individual abilities to "see" with the mind. The senses see what is, the mind sees what to do. Judgment goes beyond the empirical data gathered by the senses. Judgment is the mind's ability to come up with the correct action.

The known levels of simulation learning form a hierarchical structure. There is no way to skip levels without putting the trainee at risk and wasting the money invested in simulation.

At some point during simulation learning, training weaves over into screening of candidates. The screening may be made for a simple ranking of candidates or the washout of candidates. Screening is not valid until the candidates have all the base information and have progressed through most of the simulator program. Screening at early stages of a simulation program is nothing more than checking the cognitive speed of a candidate to retain and act on information.

Cognitive speed is the most central thing measured in intelligence tests. If you are going to screen based on initial cognitive speed, do it with an entrance IQ test. Keep a few things in mind:

- Cognitive speed is not impressive unless the IQ is 130 or higher.

- Only 2 percent of the population scores above 130.

- The other 98 percent of us with lower IQ scores can learn just as well (taking a little longer), but once we have learned something we know it as well, and can recall it as well, as those with an IQ of 130 and above.

- Judgment and IQ are related. Yet, having an IQ lower than 130 does not necessarily mean poor judgment, nor does having an IQ of 130 or higher mean good judgment.

Now that we know the management of the learning levels and uses of simulation, let's address the quality of simulation. How well can a simulator or simulated event teach and screen?

## Fidelity Management

Simulation is a training episode. It is not reality. It is an attempt to reflect our perception of reality, and it is always less than reality. The question is, How much less will you accept? Fidelity is almost another word for validity. If a picture is taken of something, how valid, accurate, is the picture? If it's 90 percent accurate, is that adequate?

Fidelity is a bit more than validity because it concerns a moving picture of a sequence of events that still photography cannot capture. Do you want blood spurting, smoke rolling, noise at the actual level, cockpit rolling? What will you accept as fidelity?

The first step in fidelity management is to adopt a philosophy. (You may change it, but adopt one. See chapter 11 for philosophy development.) There are always three possibilities.

- *Basic training is enough.* Anything more is too costly. Give them the basic systems, and they can learn the rest on the job.

- *Simulation training is never a perfect replication.* To make it so robs from the learning event; you need to be able to selectively emphasize what is important. Cover the major systems, and make sure the coverage is a good reflection of the real world.

- *Simulation training must be an exact replication.* Anything less is a threat to the entire project.

For the sake of discussion, let's accept the middle philosophy. Simulation is never perfect, but let's make it as worthwhile as possible. The practice of fidelity testing fits into any of the philosophies; how the results of fidelity tests are judged depends on which philosophy is adopted.

Fidelity testing is simply a matter of comparing what your simulator or simulation does in relation to the real world and developing fidelity tests. The procedure is simple, but hard work. Here are the steps:

- Develop a list of all systems and system interactions that are simulated.

- Go to the real world and record the systems when they are working in perfect order and during each stage of malfunctioning.

- Bring the real world data back to the simulator or simulated environment and compare.

- List the discrepancies.

- Judge the acceptability or unacceptability of the differences.

- Design remedies.

- Ensure the fixes work.

With a part-task simulation that mimics a few systems, the steps could be carried out in an afternoon. In a major nuclear power plant, the process could take years; indeed, it becomes ongoing. Beware of contracts with the actual supplier of the hardware (like missiles) where a change in hardware is contractually a basis for changes in the simulation. Trust is one thing, fidelity is another. Run your own tests.

All changes must be justified, budgeted, and documented. You must have a procedure system and a records system for the simulation (chapters 4 and 5), which must be utilized (chapters 8 and 9) and evaluated (chapters 12 and 13).

There is no answer to the question, How much simulation is enough? There is an answer to how much is too little and not accurate enough. The answer is in your mind. You have to answer it; no one else will until there is a training-related accident. To be a good fidelity manager, you have to have a certain amount of built-in distrust in yourself and your management system.

## Additional Uses of Simulation

Besides training, there are other uses of a simulated environment:

- Testing new hardware.

- Testing new software.

- Testing new emergency immediate-action drills.

- Testing transfer people who are supposed to know it all.

Simulation is the greatest innovation to ever happen to training. Its potential is unlimited.

Simulation training is a way of thinking. It offers a twenty-million-dollar machine, an empty field, a passenger jet on the end of a runway held by imaginary terrorists. Never turn fidelity management over to anyone. It's your responsibility. Use your own judgment.

# 15
# Simulation Scenario Development

A scenario is to simulation as a unit of instruction (chapter 2) is to a classroom. Simulation is a higher level of learning than occurs in a classroom and requires the greater flexibility and capability of well-designed scenarios. From the first fourteen chapters, you have gained a foundation for scenario development.

This chapter presents ways to develop quality simulation scenarios. You will need to understand the concept of a scenario, how to match learning goals to levels of simulation, scenario traps, a scenario development model, scenario format specifications, and scenario control.

## Concept of Scenario

Scenario is another concept from the ancient Romans. The root word was *scaena*, which means scene, as in a play. Its meaning was doubled when the word was expanded to *scaenarium*, a scene on a stage:

| SCEN | | ARIO |
|------|------|------|
| ↓ | | ↓ |
| SCENE | ON | STAGE |

It is a common word in the entertainment business. It's used to describe anything from an outline or synopsis of a play to the shooting script for a motion picture. A shooting script is not a bad way to think of a simulation scenario. It includes the stage (simulated environment), the scene (event and chain of events), and the characters (trainees). The shooting of the script requires recording (evaluation and critique devices). The director occasionally shouts "cut" (freeze), "let's walk through it before we go for another take" (setback, forward in slow time), and "let's skip over that and go to the main scene" (fast forward to the main event). The director (instructor) and actors (trainees) are no better than the shooting script (scenario). Let's examine the possible learning goals for scenario development.

## Matching Learning Goals and Levels

There are seven hierarchical learning levels in the use of simulation:

1. Orientation
2. Theory application
3. Single-system operation
4. Systems integration operation
5. Normal operation
6. Off-normal operation
7. Retraining and continuing training

For each level there will be several scenarios. Each scenario has a specific learning goal. Learning goals can be classified into a generic hierarchical list:

1. Familiarization
2. Identification
3. Manipulation
4. Integration

5. Operation
6. Diagnostics
7. Judgment

Figure 42 is a matrix of the two lists. The matrix allows you to classify and organize all the possible scenarios that are or could be developed. For your type of simulation, however, you may need to place Xs in different places in the matrix than they are in figure 42. The matrix also gives you a way to articulate the scenarios with the progression of the trainees through the hierarchical levels of simulation. In addition, the matrix is a management tool to use in the logical development of cost-effective scenarios and a curriculum tool to use in organizing the scenarios for effective and efficient delivery.

The matrix also makes one simple but brilliant point: effective simulation is arranged around what a simulator can do and logical levels of progressive learning. But, to ensure its effectiveness, you must protect simulation from some scenario traps.

## Scenario Traps

Beware of people who develop and present scenarios without using your matrix or some similar classification scheme based on levels of simulation interfaced with levels of learning. They devise scenarios for odd reasons that can put trainees at risk because too much bronzing, melting, and rebronzing must occur. A training situation then develops in which the trainees have to learn in spite of the scenarios, the instructors, and the simulator.

- Sole-instructor experience-based scenarios are the most dangerous. When the instructor was in the field, an unforgettable event occurred. The instructor, disregarding all the required ordering of

**SIMULATION SCENARIO MATRIX**

| Levels of Learning | Learning Goals: Familiarization | Identification | Manipulation | Integration | Operation | Diagnostics | Judgment |
|---|---|---|---|---|---|---|---|
| Orientation | X | | | | | | |
| Theory Application | X | X | | | | | |
| Single-System Operation | | X | X | | X | | |
| Systems Integration Operation | | | X | X | X | | |
| Normal Operation | | | X | X | X | | |
| Off-Normal Operation | | | X | X | X | X | X |
| Retraining/ Continuing Training | | | X | X | X | X | X |

Figure 42. Matrix of learning levels and learning goals for simulator scenarios.

learning material, will develop and teach that one scenario a dozen different ways. It may be an atonement for a sin. A bigger sin is to allow it to occur out of sequence and to the point of overkill.

- A major "industry event," such as a severe accident, can end up being blanketed over an entire series of scenarios. Although much can be learned from catastrophe, when it overpowers the content and organization of scenarios, it becomes another catastrophe waiting to happen.

- Simulator-based scenarios are where people look at a simulator from an engineering viewpoint and ask "What can we teach?" That question has to be asked, but it must be preceded or followed by "What do the trainees need to learn and when?"

There are other traps, but these are the major ones. If you take a simulated environment and rip its learning potential out, you build in future accidents. Let's look at the correct way to develop scenarios.

## Scenario Development Model

All instructional materials development models work about the same way: inputs, integration, and outputs. Scenario development requires a sliding scale on inputs, which takes a bit of explaining.

At the initial levels of simulation training, the inputs are mainly the job task analysis (chapter 2). As training progresses up the scale, the job task analysis becomes less prominent. Study the movement in the matrix (figure 42) toward full operation and introduction of system malfunctions. As you move up the scale, job task analyses, which tie neatly to measurable learning objectives, can no longer dictate what you want the trainees to be able to perform. Even when a task begins with "operate," it can either be accomplished in a wham-bang fashion or with a certain degree of style, touch, boardsmanship, and finesse; and the job task analysis can't describe that difference. And when instructional needs move to judgment, the highest level of learning, the job task analysis and measurable objectives become dangerous. If they are followed strictly, the learning and evaluation are limited to only the countable, exactly measured world, which has little to do with judgment.

At the initial levels of simulation training, the learning goals can be quite specific (identify, name, list, locate). At higher levels of simulation learning, there is a mixture of directions to locate, operate, and evaluate. (How do you write down how to evaluate an operation? To evaluate within X time? Is that realistic?) At the upper end of the scale, the learning goals become more a statement of art: bring the system up, diagnose the problem, and put it in a safe state of operation or shut it down. Measurable objectives can't deal with judgments, only things you can count. Yet, you can record judgments and evaluate the judgments by matching them against your own judgment.

The scenario development model in figure 43 is a proven model, although it does not reflect the correlation between level of learning and level of learning goal. Let's examine each block in figure 43.

43.1 *Task analysis.* A job analysis is the systematic dissection of the job for the purpose of determining the skills and supportive knowledges required to be successful on the job. It identifies each task, the steps in that task, and the skills and knowledges required to perform each task (chapter 2).

43.2 *Events, accidents.* Every business, industry, and profession has its Pearl Harbor. There are mini–Pearl Harbors

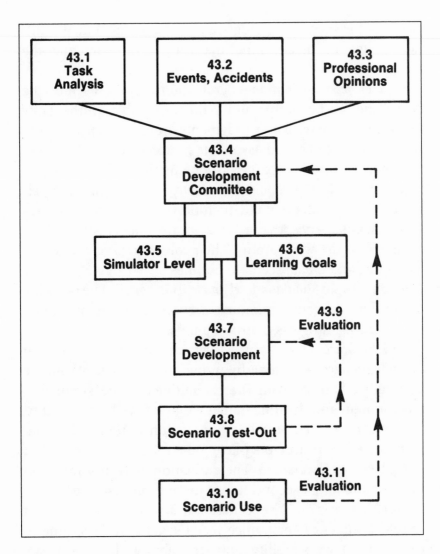

Figure 43. Scenario development model.

everyday. Sadly, many are never reported. Sadly, the ones reported are blown out of proportion by the media and sanitized by the organization. For HRT, there is always the issue of whether it is a people problem, a system problem, or a combination problem. Events and accidents are fertile

grounds for identifying elements for scenarios, but the difficulty lies in determining the truth and extracting the
teachable parts.

43.3 *Professional opinions.* Professional opinions must be
determined to be as true and valid as possible. Authenticity
is essential. These expert judgments are elicited from experienced individuals and assimilated into elements of instruction by a common sense, get-it-done method.

43.4 *Scenario Development Committee.* The Scenario Development Committee should include the instructors, the instructional supervisor, the work group supervisor, and an
expert from the work group. Their role is to sort, categorize,
catalogue, and create scenario outlines.

43.5 and 43.6 *Simulator level and learning goals.* The outcome
of the development committee, scenario outlines, is guided
by the levels and goals matrix (figure 42).

43.7 *Scenario development.* Development—the fleshing out
of each scenario—is done by individual instructors who are
thoroughly familiar with the capabilities of the simulation
environment and the time frames (hours, days) of availability.

43.8 *Scenario test-out.* The test demonstration is best accomplished by instructors playing the roles of trainees.

43.9 *Test-out evaluation.* The evaluation of the test may lead
to a revision and a second test or to multiple test-outs.

43.10 *Scenario use.* The scenario is put to work. All scenarios
should be tracked for trainee reaction and success, time to
run, instructor operability, and teachability of the scenario.
(Is the scenario worth the time it takes?)

43.11 *Scenario evaluation.* The items tracked, along with
trainees' critiques and instructor's critique, are fed back
periodically to the Scenario Development Committee for
review and recommendations.

## Scenario Format Specifications

HRT functions tend to develop one of three types of formats. There are the people who prefer a horizontal-page format. They turn a sheet sideways, divide it up and down with lines, and under obscure headings pencil in computer hieroglyphics. The second type prefers a manuscript approach that requires the line-by-line reading of several pages before the initiating conditions can be identified. The third group works from the backs of envelopes.

The point is that there is no endorsed format for scenarios. None has been around long enough to have withstood the test of time. There are, however, some specifications that dictate certain components.

*Cover sheet.* The cover sheet shows approval of the scenario by HRT and the work group. It also identifies the scenario by title, number, effective date, level of simulation, training goal, duration, and task numbers (chapter 2) of the tasks taught.

*Instructor guide sheets.* These sheets provide a brief (one-paragraph) description of the scenario, special logistics required (tools, equipment, coordination), references the instructor should review before directing the scenario, where the scenario starts (the officer is approaching the car) and where the scenario ends (suspect placed in police van). Computerized simulation requires detailed information on start points for each involved system. For scenarios that could in any way endanger the trainees or instructors, the guide sheets should provide detailed safety warnings and immediate action to be taken in case of injury. Directions should also be provided on instructor action to be taken if the scenario has to be canceled (for whatever reason) before it is completed.

*Trainee briefing sheets.* These sheets are a must to ensure that the trainees are informed of the purpose of the scenario and their expected roles. As the level of simulation increases with the training goals, the briefing sheets become less specific.

*Instructor scenario sheets.* The "shooting script" for the director, the format of scenario sheets becomes specific to each HRT function. It indeed may be an outlined script, logic charts, the sidewise page, or a series of photographs with explanations. There are two components the script must contain. Time points for instructor action is the first. These may be specific ("At 1 minute 29 seconds into scenario initiate communications malfunction") or a bit more general ("Approximately halfway through, disable the radio"), depending on the simulated environment. The second thing the script must contain is recommended evaluation points for the instructor ("Check at 2 minutes into the scenario to determine if communications malfunction has been identified").

*Trainee evaluation and critique sheets.* These sheets are the official feedback to the trainees and become part of the official records system (chapter 5). Multiform sheets are handy. The format needs to allow adequate space to write in comments. There can be general rating scales built in for communications, presence of mind, cooperation, and so on. As an official form, it requires all the typical headings, numbers, dates, and signatures.

Scenarios may vary according to the simulated environment, but certain specifications must exist in each scenario to promote effective learning. Written scenarios must also be controlled.

## Scenario Control

Scenarios, as documents, are controlled just as units of instruction are (chapters 2 and 5). The originals reside in Records and have pedigree files. The open question is, Do the trainees need to have a copy of the scenario (or a portion of it), and if so, when? It's an open argument. Let's look at three viewpoints:

- At the beginning of simulation training, each trainee receives a binder of all scenarios (without specific malfunction times).

- At the beginning of simulation training, each trainee receives a folder containing briefing sheets and a schedule.

- At the beginning of simulation training, each trainee receives a page of titles and a schedule.

What do you think? Tip: Initially, the purpose of simulation is to train. Thus, the more prior information and preparation, the better the learning. Toward the end, the purpose of simulation becomes to evaluate and screen, and advance information should be less specific.

Scenarios are the instructional vehicles for simulation. Their creation, format, and control is more an art than a plug-in-the-numbers scientific approach. To exploit the learning and evaluation capabilities of a simulated environment, you must use judgment in designing scenarios and in evaluating trainees.

# 16
# Simulation Instruction Methods

Simulation provides the opportunity for capstone training for persons in high-risk jobs. The key word is opportunity. Although simulation instructors use traditional methods of training, they can only exploit the training capabilities of simulation if they also use additional methods. Effective instruction in the simulator requires instructional techniques that are just as advanced as the simulated environment. To achieve that competency requires not only a base of typical "train-the-trainer" skills but also advanced training on sophisticated oral-questioning techniques.

This chapter presents ways of increasing the effectiveness of simulator instruction. You must know both traditional instructional methods and the question-mapping technique (QMT), and you must be able to match QMT to levels of instruction.

## Traditional Instruction Methods
In the simulated environment, instructors use traditional methods. From a time-and-motion viewpoint, more than 80

percent of instructors' behaviors can be accounted for under the following headings:

- *Demonstrating.* Instructor performs activities as a role model.

- *Minilecture.* Instructor gives definitive instruction to a group.

- *Tutoring.* Instructor gives definitive instructions to a trainee, usually one-on-one.

- *Coaching.* Instructor gives suggestions or advice on possible procedures, usually during a scenario involving little or no questioning from the instructor.

- *Drill questioning.* Instructor conducts repetitive questioning on systems, procedures, communications, manipulations, and safety.

- *Managing the scenario.* Instructor tasks include setting up the scenario, prescenario briefing of trainees, and scenario operation (introduction of malfunctions, freeze, setback, etc.).

- *Observing.* Instructor watches trainees (or tracks them) and gives neither suggestions nor advice. Instructor may or may not take notes or record the trainees on video- or voice-tape. Instructor may or may not utilize built-in time recording devices in the simulator's software.

- *Critiquing.* Instructor gives feedback to trainees on their performance after a scenario.

Which of the instructors' behavior categories provides the highest potential to cause the trainees to learn? When interacting with an instructor, when do you learn the most? When do you have to force the integration of what you know?

Certainly, things are learned when an instructor is demonstrating, giving a specific minilecture on something the trainee is about to operate, and is coaching and tutoring. During a critique, trainees will learn what they did wrong, maybe become a bit embarrassed in front of their peers. That experience can cause some learning (some of it negative). Most certainly, trainees learn when they are manipulating controls and procedures. Yet, is that when people learn the most?

The organization and reorganization of bronzing and keeping the memory trails open occurs most effectively and efficiently during periods of high interaction. Besides the interaction of trainee to simulation, there is trainee-to-instructor interaction. Oral questioning is the tool to promote the most effective interaction.

Oral questioning has the highest payback in trainee learning of any instructor behavior in the simulated environment. Here are the reasons:

- In even the simplest scenario, a trainee may do the right thing for the wrong reason. That "wrongness" could be transferred to another situation and cause an incorrect reaction that could result in disaster. The only way to find out why a trainee does something is to ask.

- The ordering of the information bits in the neurons into correct memory traces is aided by having the current traces challenged by oral questioning.

- The assimilation of several memory traces into now-needed traces to solve a new problem is aided by oral questions that force the integration of different facts and theories. Questioning makes the brain keep the trails open to the traces and use them to extract what's needed.

- The constant use of oral questioning can strengthen the built-in supervisor in the mind. In a sense, the supervisor picks up the habit of always questioning what's going on, just as a hard-questioning instructor would.

Oral questioning has benefits in addition to increasing trainee learning and retention. These fall under various categories of curriculum content evaluation, training management, and trainee screening:

- Oral questioning can identify incorrect content that was presented in earlier stages of training. The simulator instructor has the responsibility to feed that information back to the classroom instructors.

- There are different styles of thinking. Some people just do not fit into a high-risk environment. They fold under fatigue, stress, boredom between manipulations; do not pay attention to detail; and go into a daydreaming state at the wrong times (we all have to daydream). Oral questioning can assist in identifying the people of that nature. They are not lesser people; they would just do better somewhere else, and the organization could better invest its training dollars. Training management has a responsibility to feed back that information to the group that performs initial screening. There is always a need for better up-front screening.

- During the end-of-program screening (simulation progresses from training, to training and evaluation, to evaluation), oral questioning becomes the tool that provides elements of proof of the competency, or lack of competency, in a trainee. Wash-out boards need specific evidence for the protection of all involved.

There is one more thing to add about the benefits of oral questioning: it is cheap. Not much money is required to train the instructor, and oral questioning will move a beginning instructor to a fully usable instructor at a faster rate than other approaches. Let's get into the meat of oral questioning.

## Question-Mapping Technique

Oral questioning is not limited to the drill questioning period of simulation instruction. It can be used during demonstration, minilectures, tutoring, coaching (to a degree), and the critique stage. It is a versatile, effective, and economical tool. The following is a taxonomy of the questions that experienced simulator instructors typically ask:

- *Fact.* The trainee has a base of core information and draws other basic information from the environment (dials, gauges, charts, and observation). The instructor's questions deal with the basics—rules, specifications, definitions, functions, simple formulas and calculations—and information gained from the simulation (e.g., What are the rules? What should the temperature be? What does this switch operate?).

- *Theory.* The trainee has a collection of abstract thoughts about how and why systems work and function. The instructor's questions require the trainee to deal with those abstractions by supplying information beyond what is occurring or available within the simulated environment (e.g., How does this operate? Why is the temperature rising? What do you expect to happen? Why?).

- *Situation.* The trainee integrates facts—core knowledge and environmental readings—with theory.

The instructor's questions concern the big picture (e.g., What is happening? What is the problem?).

- *Procedure.* The trainee has to take an action. The instructor's questions concern what and how (e.g., What is the procedure? How do you activate this system?).

- *Judgment.* The trainee is in a simulated condition of mixed messages data, and procedures no longer give the right answers. The instructor's questions concern following the trainee's logic (e.g., What's your evaluation of the situation? Why? Why are you taking that action? What's your rationale? Are you now in a safe situation? Why? Why not?).

Two other types of oral questions occur in simulated environments. Clarification is common; it is a follow-up when the instructor is not satisfied. Rhetorical questions are those to which an answer is not expected. The purpose of a rhetorical question is to gain trainees' attention, to start them thinking along a specific line, before the real questioning gets underway. The five types of questions—fact, theory, situation, procedure, and judgment—are hierarchical. Situation and procedure questions may be close together on a scale, but overall the hierarchy of the question categories is from simple to exceptionally difficult, In chapter 15, we integrated levels of simulation learning and learning goals into a matrix, figure 42. Those two lists were also structured in a hierarchy from simple to complex. Review that matrix with the hierarchy of questions in mind. Where do fact questions, judgment questions reasonably fall? Where should you use all levels of questions?

If you visit enough simulators, observe enough simulator instructors at work, one conclusion will strike you as absolutely obvious: Instructors need significant help in relating levels of questions to levels of simulation learning and levels of learning goals. Instructors who only ask factual questions to a trainee in the off-normal/diagnostic cell or the judgment/retraining cell (figure 42, chapter 15) are wasting the resource simulation offers. Similarly, to pin trainees to the wall with procedure and judgment questions in the orientation/familiarization cell and theory application/identification cell is a sin against learning.

Although both examples are extreme, you can see it every hour in some of the most sophisticated simulated environments in the world. Millions are spent for hardware and software, but not one cent for common sense. Why? Because the instructors are teaching as they were taught. They may have learned in spite of how they were taught. As a professional HRT manager, you have the economic responsibility to get every unflawed "training product" off the assembly line and into service. Bad instruction is an inadequate reason for failure to meet your cost-effective mandate. Furthermore, you have the responsibility to allow no one to skate by the end purpose of simulation instruction, evaluation of judgment.

There is a disturbing trend occurring in full-scope simulation to isolate the instructors from the trainees during all the stages—to turn instructors into mere observers, remove their interaction from the environment, and have them become data reporters. With some untrained instructors that approach may not be a bad idea. Trainees will learn more, however, from interacting with the simulator and the instructor than from just interacting with the simulator.

One way to help your simulation program increase in efficiency and effectiveness is to implement QMT. Hard work is required for instructors to change their ways, and training management must make a commitment to improving instruction. The implementation steps are short and to the point:

1. Teach the instructors the levels of simulation learning and learning goals (figure 42, chapter 15). Point out current problems. Note advantages to matching.

2. Teach the hierarchy of questions, from facts to judgments. Show how it interrelates with figure 42. Give plenty of examples. Show how orderly questions benefit students (more learning) and the instructor (better evaluations and critiques).

3. Teach them how to classify questions. The best way is by reviewing videotapes of instructors in action. Practice is needed.

4. Teach them how to back down or escalate a question. (Begin at appropriate level with questions, for example, situation, and regress to theory and then to fact, to find the holes; or escalate, to see how much more the trainees know.)

5. Teach the flexibility of QMT. It is not predetermined dry questions, but a tool to work with each individual who is at a specific stage of training.

6. Record the instructor teaching, using voice tape, videotape, or observation. Critique the instructor. Drill the instructor. Move the instructor into a self-monitoring role.

7. Ensure QMT becomes second nature by personal observations and recording instructor's use of the method. Reward use.

QMT simplifies the role of being a simulation instructor. It takes some of the pressure off by giving a scientific hierarchy to questioning. It forces a logical sequence to learning by questioning. It aids efficiency and effectiveness by lining up questions with the ways people learn. QMT gives instructors an out when asked by trainees (who may outrank them), "Why did you ask all that?" "QMT procedure" is the answer. There is another side payment. Once instructors start using QMT, they will have to do more research to ask good questions. They will grow past only asking questions about events they have experienced.

Figure 44 is a recording instrument for QMT. It is not sophisticated, but in a given observation period, it reflects the number of each type of question asked. You can easily develop software for a microcomputer that will provide a time-based printout. Note: There is an additional type of question shown in the form, unclassified, questions that cannot be placed in one of the other seven categories. Marks in that block tend to go away as recording ability increases. However, if one instructor continually has a high percentage of marks in that block, supervisory assistance may be required. Also, the observers need not be technical experts in your training field. As a matter of fact, sometimes you would do better to have observers who only know QMT. They don't get caught up in the content of the questions.

QMT can be implemented in about three months. Each instructor should be observed initially for about five hours. Another five to ten hours is spread over the three months. A not unusual situation is to see the number of questions asked increase from ten or so an hour to close to forty per hour in highly intense training periods and critiques. You and the instructor have to judge whether the questions fit the need.

| Instructor Name | Observer Name | Date | Time — From-To |
|---|---|---|---|

| Scenario Title | Number | Simulation Level | Learning – Goal Level |
|---|---|---|---|

Directions: Every time the instructor asks a question, identify what type of question it is using the categories listed below (see key). Record each question by putting a tick mark (√) in the center section on the appropriate line. At the end of the observation session, tally each line and enter the total in the column on the right. Add the totals for a grand total at the bottom.

| TYPES OF QUESTIONS* | | TOTALS |
|---|---|---|
| Fact | | |
| Theory | | |
| Situation | | |
| Procedure | | |
| Judgment | | |
| CLARIFICATION | | |
| Rhetorical | | |
| Unclassified | | |
| | GRAND TOTAL | |

*Key:  Fact: Rules, specifications, functions, formulas.
　　　 Theory: Why and how things work.
　　　 Situation: What's going on? Where are we?
　　　 Procedure: What actions to take and how.
　　　 Judgment: What's your evaluation?
　　　 Clarification: Follow-up for verification.
　　　 Rhetorical: No answer expected.
　　　 Unclassified: Does not fit other categories.

| Printed Instructor Name | Signature | Date |
|---|---|---|

| Supervisor's Signature | Title | Date |
|---|---|---|

END

Figure 44. Question-mapping technique.

Simulated environments for learning are no better than the instruction. Instruction requires basic and advanced techniques for interacting with trainees. QMT—where the logic of learning, simple to complex, is matched to levels of simulation learning and learning goals—increases the effectiveness and efficiency of learning by simulation.

Although simulation is used in many types of training, simulation and HRT go hand-in-hand. Simulation offers the best way to provide capstone training of the highest quality to persons whose work means lives lost or saved. Simulation is thus a vital way to carry out the delivery of HRT.

But, bear in mind that you can easily have a multimillion-dollar simulator and not have the benefits of an effective HRT program. Or, you may have an empty room, shop, or field where you conduct simulation training and have a total HRT program. The concluding chapter provides guidance on ways to implement HRT and obtain the level of productivity needed.

# 17

# Conclusion: Implementation and Emerging Trends

Strategies abound for introducing change in organizations. Some strategies advocate conducting detailed research to identify opinion leaders. Another strategy involves building groups of constituents. Still others emphasize planning to the point that work is never accomplished. There may be a place and time for such efforts, but the simplest way is the best way with HRT.

This concluding chapter demonstrates a basic business way to estimate the opportunity of gaining budget support and ways to document the benefits of HRT. Throughout the chapter, labor force data are presented that document an increasing need for HRT methods. These data should provide an increased impetus for your organization to put HRT into action, an action that in turn will build broad-based support for an HRT training function that is deftly managed with precision and enthusiasm.

Enthusiasm is the key to the implementation and management of HRT. Enthusiasm, in this case, does not mean cheerleading. It means vitality, a strength that comes from having a commitment to the current and future state of trainees' competencies. Such a commitment must be sustained by a realistic philosophy of work and the role of training, a holistic philosophy that moves with the times and recognizes that now is the time for HRT methods to be implemented in training programs.

For HRT does no good on your shelf. People who are at risk, who can put others at risk, or who can place data and things in a loss-potential category need HRT. Effective HRT processes protect individuals and the organization. As a highly controlled way of performing training, HRT causes the most needed knowledges and skills to be taught, evaluated, and applied on the job. The exactness of HRT curriculum planning, review cycles for instructional materials, and directly related evaluations make HRT ultimately fair to trainees, trainers, and the organization.

There is little doubt about the competencies of trainees who successfully complete an HRT program or about the fairness of the program to those who fail. Competencies and fairness are two important characteristics of HRT that, along with flexibility, are rapidly becoming critical characteristics. Flexibility exists in HRT because of the approach used to develop curriculums. Job modifications can quickly be reflected in the training programs by simply changing the race track. The continually updated job, construct, and risk analyses allow you to be exceptionally flexible in articulating courses.

The benefits of proving *competencies*, *fairness*, and *flexibility* are reasons enough to implement HRT today. These program characteristics will be in even greater demand tomorrow because of evolving changes in the labor force. Training is big business today, and it will become an even bigger business. This chapter offers some strategies on how to begin implementing HRT by probing your current level of dissatisfaction with training, showing one way to conduct a change-potential survey, describing three implementation approaches, and presenting a way to format the executive summary of an implementation plan.

HRT is not inexpensive. Neither is losing people, data, and things. The latter portion of this chapter provides current labor force data and projections that zero in on why, starting today, you must develop a training program that makes trainees prove competencies and is unchallengeable in its fairness, while retaining realistic flexibility. The supply and demand of labor are about to run together, head-on. If you could step forward a few years in time, you would not recognize your work force. The solutions that need to be put into place will become your training challenges.

Let's begin addressing these challenges by assessing your current situation. There is no easy way to probe this area. The questions are hard, sometimes embarrassing, and might make you uncomfortable. If so, they are the right questions.

## Current Training Status

The bottom-line question in this area is, "Are you dissatisfied enough to work for change?" Are you tired of having people apply for training jobs because they think the work is easy? HRT cannot be done by just anyone. If you had HRT in place, you would have specific job competencies against which you could match job applicants' skills. You would have firm job descriptions and specific job interview questions. Then, you could judge an applicant's current competencies and development potential as an HRT training professional.

Are you satisfied with the current organizational status of training? Do senior managers and work group supervisors ignore your training schedules? Is training viewed as a second-class organization with a minor role? Are you frequently asked to put on a training program yesterday (carrying the message that training is simple and requires little preparation)? Do you have trouble justifying your budget because you cannot show empirical contributions to the organization? Do staff cuts hit training first? If you had HRT in place, the curriculum development process would pull work group supervisors into the entire planning process. They would learn the complexities of training and become friends and supporters of training. The evaluation systems HRT uses would present empirical evidence to senior management of the solid contributions training makes to the organization.

Do trainees come to training expecting a day off? Do they make fun of the instructors during breaks? Do they see little use for training? If you had HRT in place, the trainees would be learning current *must-know* skills and knowledges and be soundly tested on their learning. They would not only know they had been through a period of learning, but they would be ready to trust and apply what they had learned.

Is training making a satisfactory contribution to safety? What are your accident rates? Are accidents an accepted part of doing business? How about damaged equipment or lost data? What have these mistakes cost your organization in the last year? Are these costs acceptable? If you had HRT in place, your losses would be fewer. Training becomes a solution, not a problem. To cause that to happen means you have to take the first leadership step. You must conduct a change-potential survey of your organization.

## Change-Potential Survey

The purpose of a change-potential survey is to estimate the chance you have of introducing HRT with adequate budget support. The first step is to identify the position of your macro-organization in its life cycle. There are three possibilities shown in figure 45. Startup means just what it says, the

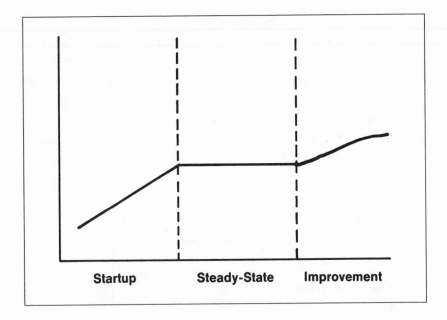

Figure 45. Organization life cycle.

organization is getting started. After such an experience, the organization seeks a period of extreme stability, or steady state. Then, the organization begins to implement slow and steady improvement. Where are you? In startup, you can implement the entire package. In steady-state, you can only plan. In the improvement stage, you can implement one process or program at a time.

The second step in your survey is to identify the acceptance of change by the senior decision makers who control the budget using three categories: below average, average, or above average. More likely than not, the successful senior decision makers will fall into the average category. Persons who are too conservative or too change-oriented tend to eventually fail as senior decision makers. The conservative ones last longer than the continuous-change-oriented ones.

Although there are supposedly several tests to determine someone's change orientation, simply make a flat judgment: below average, average, or above average. Monitoring the environment can determine where senior decision makers fall in this classification. Where is the money allocated for change going? Are no changes allowed, as opposed to everything being changed? Look around. Now you can fill in the matrix, figure 46. The cells cross. Where are you?

| | | Life-Cycle Stage | | |
|---|---|---|---|---|
| | | **Startup** | **Steady-State** | **Improvement** |
| **Senior Decision Maker** | **Below Average** | | | |
| | **Average** | | | |
| | **Above Average** | | | |

Figure 46. Change matrix.

What is the lay of the land? Is it go or no go? Remember one fact of human nature. People are born with the inclination to experiment and innovate. This trait makes our species (one of the weakest on earth) the masters of the earth, sky, and surface of the water. That spark always burns. Sometimes it needs to be rekindled. A good plan can accomplish that thermo-building process.

## Implementation Plan
The first step is to document the need for HRT. Where are your risks—people, data, or things? According to the National

Safety Council, each year two million workers in business and industry are involved in accidents, resulting in an average of nearly 12,000 deaths, 70,000 permanent disabilities, and 1,900,000 temporary disabilities. Certainly, these figures do not include members of the public who are killed and maimed because of the actions of those employed. What about the losses of data and things that occur too regularly in all organizations? Build your case. Identify current losses. Perform a risk assessment on potential losses (chapter 2). Come up with figures, hard data. The statement of losses and loss potential is the HRT benefit statement in your plan.

The next section of the plan is a listing of what you are proposing to change. Make these into bulleted statements (see figure 47). To do that, you have three implementation strategies to consider. Are you going to change everything at once? Are you going to change one process for all programs, like curriculum development? Or, are you going to identify one training program and implement HRT for that program, in entirety? These are the three choices: all, a central process, or a single program. What fits your situation?

The time frame of one year for implementing a major program is realistic. Three years is realistic for the change of a full-scope training function. The major hurdle is procedure development. Once procedures are established for even one program, you're on your way to a solid future.

Obviously, the bulleted one-page executive summary plan is backed up with a detailed plan where costs are realistically forecast (chapter 7) and benefits are specifically addressed. One thing is clear. You are already, in one way or another, deciding what is in the curriculum, writing instructional materials, and conducting evaluations. HRT is a way of doing it better, which has the long-term result of fewer resource losses.

---

**PROPOSED IMPROVEMENTS TO
CYCLOTRON TECH-LEVEL 1 PROGRAM**

**GOAL:**         Implementation of complete HRT methodology

**OBJECTIVE:**    Increasing the on-the-job application of critical
                 knowledge and skills

**BENEFIT:**      Reduction of component equipment damage and
                 down-time of cyclotron [be specific]

**IMPLEMENTATION STEPS:**

  • **Develop or hire curriculum development specialists**

  • **Develop procedures**

  • **Conduct HRT job, construct, and risk analyses**

  • **Convene curriculum committee**

  • **Generate program and course objectives**

  • **Develop units of instruction**

  • **Implement courses**

  • **Develop evaluation schemes**

  • **Implement evaluation schemes**

**TIME FRAME:  One Year**

**COST:**         $_____

---

Figure 47. Example of a list of proposed training improvements.

Also, on the plus side is the new positive opinion that user groups will gain of planning, conducting, and evaluating training. HRT forces everyone to plan and be involved. They learn quickly that although HRT is highly responsive, more effective training can occur when planning occurs. User groups become proud of their involvement in training and, as part of the decision-making chain, become supportive. Everyone will get their emotions into, and feel a part of, the training contribution system. That feeling of esprit de corps will be needed as you begin to address the major challenges coming your way because of changes in the labor force.

### Workforce 2000

*Workforce 2000* is the title of a 1987 publication by the Hudson Institute in Indianapolis. The Hudson Institute was founded in 1961 by the late Herman Kahn and some colleagues from the Rand Corporation. The project directors for *Workforce 2000* were William B. Johnson and Arnold E. Packer. Copies of the book, which is in the public domain, can be obtained from the U.S. Department of Labor in Washington, DC. It should be required reading for all trainers and personnel recruiters.

The sections dealing with U.S. population are of long-term interest. Consider the following:

- The population is growing more slowly than at any time since the 1930s.
- The average age of the population is rising.
- The pool of young workers entering the labor market will shrink.
- More women, proportionately, will enter the labor market.
- Minorities will be a larger share of new entrants into the labor force.
- Immigrants will represent the largest share of the increase in the U.S. population and the work force since the First World War.

Quite simply, on the supply side of labor, the following has occurred. Baby boomers, persons born between 1946 and 1964, are only having about half as many children as their parents. As a result, the number of 16- to 24-year-olds entering the labor market will fall from 23.4 million in 1987 to 21.3 million by 1995. That drop is an 8 percent downturn, and good help is hard to find now.

Another factor affecting the supply of labor is the quality, knowledge, and skill levels of labor market entrants. According to the *1987 Statistical Abstract of the United States*, published by the U.S. Department of Commerce, each year 10.6 percent of all students 14 years of age and older drop out of school. That statistic means that if you start off with a seventh grade class of 100 students only 47 remain for twelfth grade graduation. Furthermore, among the 2,400,000 who do graduate annually in the United States, 700,000 have severe reading problems. Another problem is that vocational and technical schools are typically housed in 1960s buildings with basic equipment of the same vintage.

Similar data apply to universities, except that the dropout rate is higher (sometimes 30–40 percent of freshmen classes). The number of college-age Americans will decrease by 18 percent by 1995. There will simply be fewer highly educated employees. Few occupations will be unaffected. This situation will cause shortfalls of scientists and engineers. The supply side downturn will not level out until well past the year 2000.

One other factor could further deplete the existing labor supply. Although the research is mixed, there is a trend toward earlier retirements. Some people want to exit the labor market early and enjoy as many years of healthy retirement as possible. That trend is worth monitoring. A lot of experience and productivity goes out the door when people retire early.

The supply side looks bleak. It becomes almost grim when the demand side is factored into the formula. Although new entrants into the labor market decrease by 8 percent from a 1987 base by 1995, the demand for labor will increase by 10 percent. The Bureau of Labor Statistics forecasts a moderate gross national product growth of 2.4 percent per year.

Obviously, many solutions will be put into place. Some, like sending more work overseas, are not desirable to a large number of Americans. More automation will most certainly increase the need for training. There will be not only more training, but more difficult training—more difficult for a variety of reasons:

- The existing work force is getting older. Older people are harder to teach.

- You will have a less technically aware population of new trainees. The education system is just not getting the job done. There are too many dropouts, and too little is taught to those remaining. (Statistical predictions are that fewer than 10 in 100 students entering kindergarten will graduate from college in the next sixteen years.)

- There will be an increase in non-English-speaking trainees and trainees who have English as a second language. Most will be Spanish speaking. How do you teach technical, English terms and concepts to persons who think in a language that does not have those words or sometimes not even comparable words?

- In an effort to fill employment needs, populations that have been discriminated against in the past will be courted. One obvious group is the handicapped. Ten percent of the babies born each year come with a handicap. What do you know about training the handicapped and suitable job modifications?

- There is an even more sensitive issue. It concerns minorities. As a group, inner-city black youth always have the highest unemployment rate. What do you know about training disadvantaged, inner-city blacks? It is a difficult job. They have learned survival, "street smarts." People who are street smart may have problems fitting into the behavior patterns in most companies and organizations. You have to assess the needs of the trainees.

- Although some progress has been made in the equal employment of women, the data show that Americans have done a shoddy job. Women are still underpaid, and most remain in traditional jobs. Are you willing to take the leadership in upgrading office clerks to highly skilled technicians? How would you take the leadership? What would you have to teach in addition to technical skills?

The data are clear. The hiring pool between now and the year 2000 will be made up more and more of dropouts, minorities, the handicapped, immigrants, and women. How well can you handle that challenge? Here is a thought to keep you awake at night. If you do an excellent job training these groups, other companies will be interested in bidding up their salaries and hiring them away. There is another complicating factor to make your life more interesting. The move to more automation, coupled with the overall move to service industries, will place additional burdens on your job analysis system. Analyzing data handling and monitoring jobs is more difficult than analyzing hands-on production jobs—quite a challenge.

## Meeting the Challenges

Leadership and development must occur at your level, at the top of your organization, and within professional associations and industry groups. The first major step is to support and strengthen local public and private education at all levels. As an individual, you can do some things. But to have a substantial impact requires a company commitment to equipment, software support, cooperative education with students, and summer work for teachers and professors.

The same things need to be accomplished at the national and state levels through professional organizations and industry groups. The dropout rates must be slowed, and students must become technically literate, as well as socially, culturally, philosophically, and politically literate.

The next step is your own professional development and that of your staff. What about training and retraining older employees? This concern should be an ongoing workshop and conference topic. Most state universities have programs in adult education; take a course on aging and learning. The university is a good place to pick up a course on minorities. Sensitivity training is still good. So are courses on industrial sociology and women in the workplace. The training is out there, through universities and conferences; you have to go after it and bring it back and share.

You may find yourself innovating new ways to conduct job analyses by dealing with state and county departments of vocational rehabilitation. Begin your development in this area by writing your congressional representative requesting the most currently amended copy of the Vocational Rehabilitation Act of 1973. The training services offered by the act are absolutely essential for an effective handicapped training program. And it will help the rest of your training program as well.

More . . .? There is always more to do, to think about, to prepare for, and eventually to excel in achieving. The labor supply problems are not going away. When you come up with solutions, share your solutions through professional organizations and in written articles. The hope is that others will do the same, and together trainers can contribute to the overall solution, a solution we can be a part of, rather than watch as it passes us by.

Good Luck. Have confidence in yourself and the HRT processes. As a trainer, you have the opportunity and responsibility to make things better. Remember, no matter how good or bad a situation may be, you can always make the situation better. You are not alone because you can develop a followship. They will allow you to lead them to success, a success that is founded in the past, is set in the present, and looks to the future.

# Appendix

**HIGH-RISK TRAINING PROCEDURE — INTERNAL**

*HRT Procedure Development*

| Procedure Title | Number | Effective Date |
|---|---|---|

| Approved: Signature HRT — Manager | Date of Signature | Required Review Date |
|---|---|---|

**CROSS-INDEX TITLES**

(Procedures)
(Procedure Development)
(Procedure Systems)
(Procedure Requirements)
(Procedure Tracking)
(Procedure Responsibility)
(Procedure Changes)

**SIGNATURES AND DATES OF THOSE ASSIGNED PRIMARY
RESPONSIBILITIES IN THIS PROCEDURE**

| PRINTED NAME | SIGNATURE | JOB TITLE | RESPONSIBILITY NUMBERS | DATE OF SIGNATURE |
|---|---|---|---|---|
| | | Supv., Curric./Instr. | 5.3 | |
| | | Supv., Evaluation | 5.3 | |
| | | Supv., Record/Doc. | 5.2 | |
| | | | | |
| | | | | |
| | | | | |
| | | | | |

**FORM NUMBER 3.1-1, I/E**
**PAGE 1 OF_____**

HRTP-INTERNAL, REV. 3
Page 2 of _____

1.0   INTENT
This procedure describes the development, review, distribution, and change processes for the HRT procedure system. It applies to all HRT procedures.

2.0   PHILOSOPHY
Procedures are ways to give clear directions to all who interact with a system. The directions must concisely tell the user what, when, and where to accomplish the tasks. This procedure structures that direction-giving process.

3.0   REFERENCES
3.1   *Nobels Better Manuals.* James, William E., and James M. Dewey. San Francisco: Macy Press.
3.2   *Procedure Standards.* Corsen, Terry R. Bangor, ME: National Association of HRT Professionals.

4.0   TERMINOLOGY
4.1   *Procedure.* Written directions on how to accomplish tasks.
4.2   *HRT-I Procedures.* Written directions for training staff only.
4.3   *HRT-I/E Procedures.* Written directions for training staff and external personnel who have training responsibilities.

5.0   RESPONSIBILITIES
5.1   Manager–HRT approves the need for a procedure and approves the final draft.
5.2   Supervisor, Records and Documents, manages the development and distribution system.

5.3    Supervisors–HRT must critique the responsibilities assigned and, after deliberation, carry out the negotiated responsibilities.

5.4    Staff–HRT must critique the responsibilities assigned and, after deliberation, carry out the negotiated responsibilities or exercise the professional grievance procedure (HRTP–6.3–I).

6.0    DIRECTIONS

6.1    Each procedure will have the standard cover sheet, Form No. 3.1–I/IE. The following sections will be included:

6.1.1    *Intent.* Statement of the purpose of the procedure and scope.

6.1.2    *Philosophy.* Why is this procedure being written? What is the goal?

6.13    *References.*

6.1.3.1    Include all upper-tier procedures that drive the procedure.

6.1.3.2    Include all scientific and technical references.

6.1.3.3    Include all textbook references.

6.1.4    *Terminology.* Includes all nonstandard concepts with precise definitions.

6.1.5    *Responsibilities.* An exact description of the role of each incumbent designated as a responsible party.

6.1.6    *Directions.* Specific step-by-step obligations for each responsible position.

6.1.7 *Records.* Listing of the forms required to close the procedure loops and document the completion of the directions.

6.2 Each procedure will be prepared using the following notation and pagination system:

6.2.1 All HRTPs shall be numbered by page of page and show revision number in upper left-hand corner.

6.2.2 All HRTP forms shall be included in the procedure and numbered in the lower left-hand corner, including revision number.

7.0 RECORDS

7.1 Copy of entire procedure and cover sheets to records.

7.2 Copy of all forms to records.

# Index

 Gary Ward is an industrial trainer, writer, and consultant with more than twenty years' experience in technical training and industrial education. Among his accomplishments is the development of the staff, curriculum, and facilities for the most successful commercial nuclear training center in the United States. His experience also includes military service and military training program development. He organized the Simulator Users Group for the nuclear industry and is experienced with flight, part-task, and nuclear control room simulators.

While working full-time, Gary Ward earned five college and university degrees in areas of occupational and adult learning. He continually researches how adults learn, retain, and apply technical information.

In addition to writing *High-Risk Training*, Gary Ward has had articles published in many professional journals and has authored a series of booklets. He is currently pursuing a writing career and is conducting seminars on high-risk training. Gary Ward lives in Mountaintop, Pennsylvania, with his wife Sharon and sons Justin and Cade.